# Renaissance & Reformation Biographies

# Renaissance & Reformation Biographies

Volume **1**:
A–K

**PEGGY SAARI &**
**AARON SAARI**, EDITORS
Julie Carnagie, Project Editor

Detroit • New York • San Diego • San Francisco • Cleveland • New Haven, Conn. • Waterville, Maine • London • Munich

## THOMSON
## GALE

**Renaissance and Reformation: Biographies**

Peggy Saari and Aaron Saari

**Project Editor**
Julie L. Carnagie

**Permissions**
Shalice Shah-Caldwell

**Imaging and Multimedia**
Robert Duncan, Kelly A. Quin

**Product Design**
Pamela A. Galbreath

**Composition**
Evi Seoud

**Manufacturing**
Rita Wimberly

**LIBRARY OF CONGRESS CATALOGING-IN-PUBLICATION DATA**

Saari, Peggy.
Renaissance and Reformation : biographies / Peggy Saari and Aaron Saari.
    p. cm.
Summary: Profiles fifty people who played a significant role during the Renaissance and Reformation periods, including John Calvin, Peter Paul Rubens, Catherine de Medicis, and Johannes Kepler.
Includes bibliographical references and index.
ISBN 0-7876-5470-1 (set : hardcover : alk. paper) – ISBN
0-7876-5471-X (v. 1 : alk. paper) – ISBN 0-7876-5472-8 (v. 2 : alk. paper)
1. Europe–Biography–Juvenile literature. 2. Renaissance–Biography–Juvenile literature. 3. Reformation–Biography–Juvenile literature. [1. Europe–Biography. 2. Renaissance–Biography. 3. Reformation–Biography.] I. Saari, Aaron Maurice. II. Title.
CT759 .S33 2002
940.2'1'0922–dc21
                                                                    2001008609

# Contents

# Volume 2: L–Z

# Reader's Guide

**R**enaissance and Reformation: Biographies presents the biographies of women and men relevant to the Renaissance and Reformation period in Europe. Among the fifty people profiled in each of the two volumes are artists, authors, religious leaders, musicians, scientists, and kings and queens who helped to define this ever-changing period in European history. *Renaissance and Reformation: Biographies* does not include only biographies of readily recognizable figures of the era, such as German religious leader and reformer Martin Luther, Italian artist Leonardo da Vinci, and English playwright William Shakespeare, but it also includes profiles of lesser-known people, such as Italian scholar Isotta Nogarla, the author of the first piece of feminist writing, and Jewish court official Isaac Abrabanel, who protested the persecution of Spanish Jews.

## Additional features

*Renaissance and Reformation: Biographies* also contains short biographies of people who are in some way connected with the main biographee and sidebar boxes highlighting interesting information. More than one hundred black-and-white illustrations enliven the text, while cross-references are made to other people profiled in the two-volume set. Each entry concludes with a list of sources—including Web sites—for further information for additional study, and both volumes contain a timeline, a glossary, and a cumulative index of the people and subjects discussed in *Renaissance and Reformation: Biographies*.

## Comments and suggestions

We welcome your comments on this work as well as your suggestions for topics to be featured in future editions of *Renaissance and Reformation: Biographies*. Please write: Editors, *Renaissance and Reformation: Biographies*, U•X•L, 27500 Drake Rd., Farmington Hills, MI 48331-3535; call toll-free: 1-800-877-4253; fax: 248-699-8097; or send e-mail via www.gale.com.

# Timeline of Events

**1327** Italian poet **Petrarch** begins writing *Canzoniere,* a series of love lyrics in which he departed from the medieval convention of seeing a woman as a spiritual symbol and depicted Laura as a real person.

**1451** Italian scholar **Isotta Nogarola** writes "On the Equal and Unequal Sin of Eve and Adam," which is considered the first piece of feminist writing.

**1454** German printer **Johannes Gutenberg** perfects movable type.

**1458** **Margaret of Navarre**'s *Heptaméron* is published and becomes an important work of the Renaissance period.

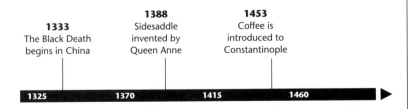

**1333**
The Black Death begins in China

**1388**
Sidesaddle invented by Queen Anne

**1453**
Coffee is introduced to Constantinople

1325     1370     1415     1460

| 1469 | Italian merchant **Lorenzo de' Medici** takes control of Florence and becomes a patron of great Renaissance artworks. |
|---|---|
| 1490s | German artist **Albrecht Dürer** raises woodcut to the level of high art. |
| 1492 | Jewish court official **Isaac Abrabanel** protests the Edict of Expulsion, which ordered all Jews to leave Spain. |
| 1494 | Pope **Alexander VI** issues the Treaty of Tordesillas that gives Portugal authority over Brazil. |
| 1494 | Italian preacher **Girolamo Savonarola** influences a new pro-French government in Florence. |
| 1495 | **Alexander VI** organizes the Holy League, an alliance between the Papal States, the Holy Roman Empire, Spain, Venice, and Milan against France. |
| 1495 | Italian painter **Leonardo da Vinci** begins the *Last Supper.* For this painting he experiments with oil-based paint, which is more easily blended, but his efforts are unsuccessful. |
| 1498 | Italian sculptor **Michelangelo** starts the *Pietà,* his first important commission. |
| 1498 | **Girolamo Savonarola** is executed for committing heresy, or violating church law. |
| 1503 | **Leonardo** begins work on the *Mona Lisa,* one of the most famous portraits in the Western world. |
| 1511 | Italian artist **Raphael** completes *School of Athens,* considered to be one of his greatest achievements. |
| 1512 | **Michelangelo Buonarroti** completes the decoration of the Sistine Chapel ceiling at the Vatican in Rome. |

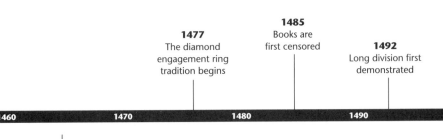

**1477**
The diamond engagement ring tradition begins

**1485**
Books are first censored

**1492**
Long division first demonstrated

1460   1470   1480   1490

**1513** Italian diplomat **Niccolò Machiavelli** writes *The Prince,* in which he proclaims his controversial political philosophy.

**1516** Dutch humanist **Desiderius Erasmus** publishes *Praise of Folly,* a satire of the Roman Catholic Church and its clergy. That same year Erasmus publishes his translation of the New Testament of the Bible, the first published Greek text.

**1516** English humanist **Thomas More** publishes *Utopia.* Modeled on Plato's *Republic, Utopia* describes an imaginary land that is free of grand displays of wealth, greed, and violence.

**1517** German priest **Martin Luther** posts his "Ninety-Five Theses," initiating the Protestant Reformation.

**1519** King Charles I of Spain is elected Holy Roman Emperor **Charles V,** leading to the spread of the Spanish empire east from Spain to include the kingdoms of Germany, Hungary, Bohemia, Naples, and Sicily. The empire also extends south and west to include possessions in North Africa and the Americas.

**1520** King **Francis I** of France meets King **Henry VIII** of England at the Field of the Cloth of Gold in order to form an alliance against Holy Roman Emperor **Charles V.**

**1520s** Swiss-born physician **Theophrastus Paracelsus** pioneers the use of chemicals to treat disease.

**1521** **Martin Luther** is declared an "outlaw of the church" by **Charles V** at the Diet of Worms.

**1521** The Ottoman Empire begins to reach its height when the sultan **Süleyman I** defeats Hungary in the Battle of Mohács.

**1506**
Christopher
Columbus dies

**1513**
First school in Puerto
Rico founded

**1520**
Chocolate
imported by Spain

1500     1510     1520     1530

**1525**    **Francis I** is captured by the Spanish at the Battle of Pavia.

**1527**    King **Gustav I Vasa** begins establishing Lutheranism in Sweden.

**1528**    French diplomat **Baldassare Castiglione** publishes *Book of the Courtier.* The book is an immediate success and quickly becomes a guide to etiquette for both the bourgeoisie and the aristocracy in Europe.

**1528**    **Albrecht Dürer's** *The Four Books on Proportions* is published. It is his last and most important theoretical work.

**1532**    King **Henry VIII** is declared supreme head of the Church of England, completing the break between England and the Roman Catholic Church.

**1534**    French author **François Rabelais** begins publishing his most popular work, *Gargantua and Pantagruel.*

**1535**    **Thomas More** is beheaded after refusing to acknowledge the Act of Supremacy that makes King **Henry VIII** supreme head of the Church of England.

**1536**    French-born Protestant reformer **John Calvin** writes *Institutes of the Christian Religion,* which outlines his beliefs and gains him attention as an important religious leader.

**1538**    **Michelangelo Buonarroti** is commissioned to redesign the Capitoline Hill in Rome.

**1540**    Spanish priest **Ignatius of Loyola** founds the Society of Jesus (Jesuits). His Jesuit order eventually becomes the single most powerful weapon of the Catholic Reformation.

**1543**    *On the Revolution of Celestial Spheres* by Polish astronomer **Nicolaus Copernicus** is published. The

**1523**
Turkeys introduced
to Europe

**1530**
The potato is
discovered

**1533**
First printing
press brought to
the Americas

1520        1525        1530        1535

book gives important information about the orbits of the planets and begins a revolution in human thought by serving as the cornerstone of modern astronomy.

1543 Belgian anatomist **Andreas Vesalius** publishes *On the Fabric of the Human Body,* one of the most important contributions to human anatomy.

1544 **Gustav I Vasa** abolishes the elective monarchy and instills a hereditary monarchy.

1547 Emperor **Charles V** defeats German Protestant princes at the Battle of Mühlberg. Charles hopes his victory will stop the spread of Protestanism throughout the Holy Roman Empire.

1547 **Michelangelo Buonarroti** directs the construction of the new Saint Peter's Basilica.

1548 **Ignatius of Loyola** publishes *Spiritual Exercises.* This short but influential book outlines a thirty-day regimen, or systematic plan, of prayer and acts of self-denial and punishment, with the understanding that devotion to God must be central.

1550s Italian architect **Andrea Palladio** popularizes the villa.

1550s Italian composer **Giovanni Pierluigi da Palestrina** creates the oratorio, a lengthy religious choral work that features recitatives, arias, and choruses without action or scenery.

1555 **John Calvin** organizes an evangelical government in Geneva, Switzerland.

1555 Italian artist **Sofonisba Anguissola** paints *The Chess Game.* This painting is meant to demonstrate female excellence at an intellectual game.

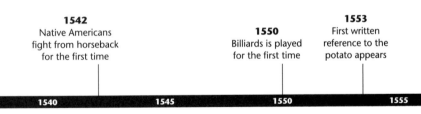

**1542**
Native Americans fight from horseback for the first time

**1550**
Billiards is played for the first time

**1553**
First written reference to the potato appears

1540     1545     1550     1555

1555    French astrologer **Nostradamus** begins publishing *Centuries*, his best-selling book of predictions.

1556    Holy Roman Emperor **Charles V** abdicates the throne after building one of the largest empires in history.

1558    **Elizabeth I** begins her forty-five-year reign as queen of England and Ireland.

1560    **Catherine de Médicis** is named regent of France after the death of her husband King Henry II.

1560s    **King Philip II** of Spain begins building the Escorial, an enormous complex of buildings north of Madrid.

1562    **Teresa de Ávila** founds the Reformed Discalced Carmelite Order.

1563    German artist **Pieter Bruegel** paints *Tower of Babel,* one of his most famous works.

1567    **Philip II** introduces the Spanish Inquisition in the Netherlands.

1570    **Andrea Palladio** publishes *Four Books on Architecture.*

1580    French author **Michel de Montaigne** publishes *Essays.* The work creates a new literary genre, the essay, in which he uses self-portrayal as a mirror of humanity in general.

1587    Queen **Elizabeth I** orders the execution of Mary, Queen of Scots after a conspiracy to assassinate Elizabeth is discovered.

1588    **Elizabeth I** reaches the height of her reign when her English naval fleet defeats the Spanish Armada.

1592    English playwright **William Shakespeare** begins his career in London and goes on to become one of the most famous playwrights in the world.

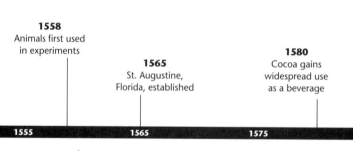

**1558**
Animals first used
in experiments

**1565**
St. Augustine,
Florida, established

**1580**
Cocoa gains
widespread use
as a beverage

1555      1565      1575      1585

1605   Spanish author **Miguel de Cervantes** publishes the first part of *Don Quixote,* one of the great masterpieces of world literature.

1606   Foremost English playwright **Ben Jonson**'s dramatic genius is fully revealed for the first time in *Volpone,* a satiric comedy that contains the playwright's harshest and most unrelenting criticism of human vice.

1609   Italian astronomer **Galileo Galilei** perfects the telescope and makes revolutionary observations of the universe.

1609   German astronomer **Johannes Kepler** publishes his first two laws of planetary motion in *New Astronomy.*

1611   King **James I** of England approves a new English translation of the Bible.

1616   The Roman Catholic Church orders **Galileo Galilei** to cease promoting the Sun-centered universe theory.

1616   Italian painter **Artemisia Gentileschi** becomes the first woman to be admitted to the Florentine Academy of Art.

1618   **Johannes Kepler** publishes his third law of planetary motion.

1620   English philosopher **Francis Bacon** publishes *New Method.*

1621   **James I** dissolves the British Parliament.

1624   German-born artist **Peter Paul Rubens** paints his famous *Self-portrait.*

1666   **Margaret Cavendish** publishes *The Description of a New World Called the Blazing World,* considered to be one of the first works of science fiction.

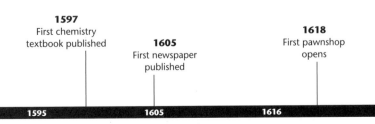

**1597**
First chemistry
textbook published

**1605**
First newspaper
published

**1618**
First pawnshop
opens

1595        1605        1616        1625

# Words to Know

**A**

**Abbey:** A church connected with a monastery.

**Abbot:** A head of a monastery.

**Abbess:** A head of a convent.

**Abdicate:** To step down from the throne.

**Absolution:** Forgiveness of sins pronounced by a priest.

**Absolutism:** The concentration of all power in the hands of one ruler.

**Adultery:** Having sexual relations with someone who is not the person's husband or wife.

**Agriculture:** The growing of crops for food and other products.

**Alchemy:** The medieval science devoted to changing common metals into gold and silver.

**Algebra:** A form of arithmetic in which letters represent numbers.

**Allegory:** A story featuring characters with symbolic significance.

**Altarpiece:** A work of art that decorates an altar of a church.

**Anatomy:** The study of the structure of the body.

**Annulment:** An order that declares a marriage invalid.

**Anti-Semitism:** Prejudice against Jews.

**Apprentice:** One who learns a craft, trade, or profession from a master.

**Aristocracy:** The upper social class.

**Armor:** A protective suit made of iron worn by a soldier in battle.

**Artillery:** Various types of weapons.

**Astrolabe:** A device used to observe and calculate the distance of celestial bodies.

**Astrology:** The study of the heavens to predict future events.

**Astronomy:** The study of celestial bodies, such as planets, stars, the Sun, and the Moon.

**Atheist:** One who does not believe in God.

**Augsburg Confession:** An official statement of Lutheran churches prepared in 1530.

**Auto da fé:** Act of faith; public expression of commitment to Christianity required of supposed heretics during the Inquisition.

**Autopsy:** The dissection and examination of a corpse to determine the cause of death.

**Axiom:** A statement accepted as being true.

## B

**Babylonian Captivity:** The name given to the period from 1307 to 1376 when the Roman Catholic pope lived in Avignon, France.

**Baptism:** A Christian ceremony in which a person is blessed with water and admitted to the Christian faith.

**Barbarism:** A lack of refinement or culture.

**Baroque:** The term used to describe the music, art, literature, and philosophy of the seventeenth century; exuberant, sensuous, expressive, and dynamic style.

**Battle of Lepanto (1571):** A sea battle in which the European Christian naval alliance defeated the fleet of the Ottoman Empire.

**Battle of Mohács (1526):** A conflict in which the Ottoman Empire conquered much of Hungary.

**Battle of Mühlberg (1547):** A conflict in which Holy Roman Emperor Charles V defeated the Schmalkaldic League.

**Battle of Pavia:** A conflict during the Italian Wars, in which Spain defeated France; it resulted in the Treaty of Madrid (1526), requiring France to give up claims to Italy, Burgundy, Flanders, and Artois.

**Battle of Preveza (1538):** A sea battle in which the Ottoman navy defeated the Genoan fleet and gained control of the eastern Mediterranean Sea.

**Bewitch:** To cast a spell over someone or something.

**Bible:** The Christian holy book.

**Biology:** The study of living organisms and their processes.

**Bishop:** The head of a church district.

**Black Death:** A severe epidemic of the bubonic plague that started in Europe and Asia in the fourteenth century.

**Blasphemy:** An expression of contempt toward God.

**Bleeding:** The procedure of draining blood from the body to cure disease.

**Bourgeoisie:** The middle class.

**Brethren of the Common Life:** The Protestant organization that founded humanist schools.

**Bull:** An order issued by a pope.

## C

**Cadaver:** A dead body used for study purposes.

**Canon:** Church law or degree; clergyman at a cathedral.

**Canonized:** Named as a saint, or a person declared holy by the Roman Catholic Church.

**Canton:** A province or state.

**Cardinal:** A Roman Catholic Church official ranking directly below the pope.

**Carnival:** A celebration of a holy day.

**Cartography:** The study of maps and map-making.

**Cartoon:** A preparatory design or drawing for a fresco.

**Castle:** The residence of a lord and his knights, family, servants, and other attendants; eventually the center for a village and local government.

**Catechism:** A book of religious instructions in the form of questions and answers.

**Cathedral:** A large Christian house of worship.

**Catholic Reformation:** The reform movement within the Roman Catholic Church of the sixteenth and seventeenth centuries; also called the Counter Reformation.

**Cavalry:** Soldiers who ride horses in battle.

**Censored:** Suppressed or prohibited, as by the church.

**Chamber music:** Music composed for performance in a private room or small auditorium, usually with one performer for each part.

**Chancellor:** A chief secretary or administrator.

**Chivalric code:** A complex system of honor observed by knights during the Middle Ages.

**Christ:** The name for Jesus of Nazareth, founder of Christianity.

**Christendom:** The kingdom of Christ; name given to Europe by the Christian church.

**Christianity:** The religion founded by Jesus of Nazareth, who was also called the Christ.

**City-state:** A geographic region under the governmental control of a central city.

**Classical period:** The ancient Greek and Roman world, especially its literature, art, architecture, and philosophy.

**Clergy:** Church officials, including bishops, priests, and monks.

**Cloister:** Walkways with an arched open side supported by columns; also a term for an enclosed monastery or convent.

**Coat of arms:** An emblem signifying noble rank.

**Commedia dell' arte:** A type of comedy performed by professional acting companies that improvise plots depending on the materials at hand and the talents of the actors.

**Commune:** A district governed by a group of leaders called a corporation.

**Communion:** A Christian religious ceremony in which bread and wine represent the body and blood of Jesus of Nazareth (Christ).

**Concordat of Bologna (1516):** The agreement in which the Catholic Church in France came under direct control of the king.

**Confession:** An admission of sins to a priest; statement of belief forming the basis of a religious faith or denomination.

**Confirmation:** The act of conferring the gift of the Holy Spirit.

**Confraternity:** A society devoted to a charitable or religious cause.

**Conscription:** The requirement of all men above a certain age to serve in the military.

**Constitution:** A document that specifies the laws of a state and the rights of its citizens.

**Consubstantiation:** The concept that bread and wine in the Christian communion service are only symbolic of the body and blood of Christ, not transformed into the actual body and blood.

**Convent:** A house for women who are dedicated to religious life; also called a nunnery.

**Conversion:** The act of leaving one religion to accept another.

*Converso:* The Spanish word for a Jew who converted to Christianity.

**Coup d'etat:** A violent overthrow of a government.

**Courtier:** A member of a court; a gentleman.

**Courtly love:** Part of the chivalric code according to which a knight undertakes a quest (religious journey) or a tournament (game of combat) dedicated to a special lady.

**Creed:** A statement of religious beliefs.

**Crucifix:** A carved image of Christ crucified on a cross.

**Crusades (1096–1291):** A series of wars waged by Christians against Muslims in an effort to recapture the city of Jerusalem in the Holy Land; also wars against other non-Christians and Christians who challenged the church.

**Curate:** A clergyman in charge of a parish.

## D

**Democracy:** A government based on the will of the majority of people.

**Dialectic:** Conversation based on discussion and reasoning.

**Dialogue:** A written work in which two or more speakers discuss a topic.

**Diet:** A meeting of representatives from states and districts in the Holy Roman Empire.

**Diet of Augsburg (1530):** A meeting in which Protestants and Catholics tried unsuccessfully to reach a compromise.

**Diet of Nuremberg (1532):** A meeting in which Protestant princes forced Emperor Charles V to continue toleration of Lutheranism indefinitely.

**Diet of Speyer (1526):** A meeting in which it was decided that each prince was responsible for settling religious issues in his own territory "until a general council of the whole Church could be summoned."

**Diet at Speyer (1529):** A meeting in which the 1526 Diet of Speyer decision was revoked; some Lutheran reformers protested, thus gaining the name "Protestants."

**Diet of Worms (1521):** A meeting in which Martin Luther refused to recant his beliefs and was declared an outlaw of the church by Emperor Charles V.

**Diocese:** A territorial district of a bishop.

**Diplomat:** A political negotiator or representative of a government.

**Disciple:** One who spreads the doctrines of a religious leader; one of the twelve followers of Jesus of Nazareth (Christ).

**Disputation:** A formal debate.

**Divine right:** The concept that a ruler is chosen directly by God.

**Doctrine:** Official church teachings.

**Doge:** The duke of Venice, Italy.

**Dowry:** Money, goods, or the estate that a woman brings to her husband in marriage.

**Ducat:** A gold coin used in various European countries.

**Duel:** A form of combat with weapons, usually pistols, between two persons in the presence of witnesses.

**Dynasty:** Rulers from the same family who hold political power for many generations.

## E

**East Roman Empire:** In the Middle Ages, the countries of eastern Europe; based in Byzantium (now Istanbul, Turkey) and formed after the split of the Roman Empire in A.D. 395; also known as the Byzantine Empire.

**East-West Schism (1052):** The splitting of the Christian church into the Eastern Orthodox Church at Constantinople and the Roman Catholic Church in Rome.

**Easter:** The commemoration of Christ's resurrection, or rising from the dead.

**Eclipse:** The total or partial obscuring of one celestial body by another, as in the eclipse of the Sun by the Moon.

**Edict of Worms:** The statement issued by Emperor Charles V at the Diet of Worms in 1521; it condemned Lutheranism in all parts of the Holy Roman Empire.

**The Elect:** A few people chosen by God to receive salvation and to lead others who are not chosen for salvation.

**Elector:** A German prince entitled to vote for the Holy Roman Emperor.

**Elegy:** A poem expressing sorrow.

**Epic:** A literary work, usually a poem, in which the main character undertakes a long journey.

**Epidemic:** A widespread outbreak of disease.

**Etiquette:** Rules for proper manners.

**Evangelism:** A personal commitment to the teachings of Jesus of Nazareth (Christ).

**Excommunicate:** The act of being expelled from membership in a church.

**Exile:** Forcibly sending a person away from his or her native country or state.

**F**

**Fable:** A story with animal characters that teaches a moral lesson.

**Facade:** The outer front wall of a building.

**Factions:** Opposing sides in a conflict.

**Faith:** The acceptance of truth without question; also a profession of religious belief.

**Farce:** Literary or theatrical work based on exaggerated humor.

**Fasting:** Abstaining from food.

**Feudalism:** The social and political system of the Middle Ages, under which rulers granted land to lords in exchange for loyalty.

**Fief:** Territory granted to a nobleman by a king or emperor under feudalism.

**First Helvetic Confession (1536):** A statement of Protestant reform goals.

**Florin:** A coin made in Florence, Italy; later used by various European countries.

**Free will:** Exercise of individual choice independent of the will of God.

**French Wars of Religion (1562–98):** Series of conflicts between Catholics and Huguenots (Protestants) in France.

**Fresco:** A wall painting made by applying paint over a thin layer of damp lime plaster.

**Friar:** A man who belongs to a religious order that takes a vow of poverty.

## G

**Galaxy:** A very large group of stars.

**Galley:** A ship propelled by oars.

**Genre:** A form of literature.

**Geography:** The study of the physical and cultural features of the Earth's surface.

**Geometry:** The branch of mathematics that deals with points, lines, angles, surfaces, and solids.

**German Peasants' War (1524–26):** Rebellion staged by peasants against Catholic princes in Germany.

**Gospel:** The word of God delivered by Jesus of Nazareth (Christ).

**Grammar school:** An elementary school; in the Renaissance, called Latin grammar school because students were required to learn Latin as the basis of the humanist curriculum.

**Great Schism (1378–1418):** The name given to a period of time when there were two Roman Catholic popes, one in Rome and one in Avignon, France.

**Guild:** An association of craftsmen, merchants, and professionals that trained apprentices and set standards of production or business operation.

## H

**Habit:** The garment worn by a nun.

**Hanseatic League:** A trading network formed in the Middle Ages among cities around the Baltic Sea and the North Sea.

**Heliocentric:** Sun-centered.

**Heresy:** Violation of church laws.

**Heretic:** One who violates or opposes the teachings of the church.

**Hermit:** A member of a religious order who retires from society and lives in solitude.

**Holy Roman Empire:** A revival of the ancient Roman Empire; established by Otto the Great in A.D. 962.

**Holy Spirit:** The third person of the Christian Trinity (God the Father, the Son, and the Holy Spirit).

**House:** A family of rulers.

**Huguenots:** French Protestants.

**Humanism:** A human-centered literary and intellectual movement based on the revival of classical culture that started the Renaissance.

**Humanistic studies:** Five academic subjects consisting of grammar (rules for the use of a language), rhetoric (art of effective speaking and writing), moral philosophy (study of human conduct and values), poetry, and history.

**Hundred Years' War (1337–1453):** A series of intermittent conflicts between England and France over the French throne.

# I

**Idolatry:** The worship of images, or false gods.

**Incarnate:** The spirit in bodily form.

**Index of Prohibited Books:** A list of books banned by the Roman Catholic Church.

**Indulgence:** The Roman Catholic Church practice of granting a partial pardon of sins in exchange for money.

**Infantry:** Soldiers trained to fight in the front line of battle.

**Inquisition:** An official court established by the Roman Catholic Church in 1233 for the purpose of hunting down and punishing heretics; during the Renaissance, it continued under the Spanish Inquisition (1492) and Roman Inquisition (1542).

**Investiture struggle:** An eleventh-century conflict between popes and rulers over the right to appoint bishops.

**Islam:** A religion founded by the prophet Muhammad.

**Italian Wars (1494–1559):** A conflict between France and Spain over control of Italy.

## J

*Janissaries:* An elite army of the Ottoman Empire, composed of war captives and Christian youths forced into service.

**Journeyman:** The stage of apprenticeship during which one travels from job to job working in the shop of a master craftsman.

**Joust:** Combat on horseback between two knights with lances.

## K

**Kabbalah:** Also cabala; system of Jewish religious and mystical thought.

**Knight:** A professional warrior who rode on horseback in combat; also known as a vassal, or one who pledged his loyalty to a lord and a king.

## L

**Laity:** Unordained church members.

**Lance:** A long polelike weapon with a sharpened steel point.

**Lent:** The forty week days prior to Easter, the celebration of Christ's rising from the dead; a time devoted to prayer, penance, and reflection.

**Limbo:** A place where the unbaptized remain after death.

**Linear perspective:** A system derived from mathematics in which all elements of a composition are measured and arranged according to a single point (perspective).

**Liturgy:** Rites and texts used in a worship service.

**Logarithms:** A system of numbers with points that move on two lines of numbers, one point on increasing arithmetic value and the other moves on decreasing geometric values.

**Loggia:** An open, roofed porchlike structure with arches that overlooks a courtyard.

**Logic:** A system of thought based on reason.

**Lord:** One who was granted a large estate by a king in exchange for loyalty.

## M

**Madrigal:** A song based on a poem or sacred text.

**Magic:** The use of spells or charms believed to have supernatural powers over natural forces; black magic is the use of evil spirits for destructive purposes; white magic is beneficial use of magic.

**Magistrate:** A government official similar to a judge; a mayor.

**Marburg Colloquy (1529):** Gathering of Protestant theologians who met to create a common creed (statement of beliefs) as a united front against Catholics.

**Martyr:** A person who voluntarily suffers death for a religious cause.

**Masque:** Court entertainment featuring masked actors, elaborate costumes, music, and dance.

**Mass:** The Roman Catholic worship service in which communion is taken.

**Medical practitioner:** An unlicensed healer who treats illness and disease.

**Medieval:** A term for the Middle Ages.

**Mercenary:** A hired soldier.

**Mercury:** A silver-colored, poisonous metallic element.

**Metallurgy:** The study and use of metals.

**Metaphysics:** The study of the nature of reality and existence.

**Meteorology:** The science that deals with the study of weather patterns.

**Middle Ages:** A period in European history that began after the downfall of the West Roman Empire in the fourth and fifth centuries and continued into the fifteenth century; once called the Dark Ages.

**Midwife:** One who assists in childbirth.

**Mistress:** A woman who has a continuing sexual relationship with a married man and is not his wife.

**Monarchs:** Kings and queens who have sole ruling power.

**Monastery:** A house for monks, members of a religious order.

**Monk:** A man who is a member of a religious order and lives in a monastery.

**Monopoly:** Exclusive control or possession of a trade or business.

**Moors:** Muslim Arab and Berber conquerors of Spain.

*Morisco:* The Spanish word for a Muslim who converted to Christianity.

**Mortal sin:** An act of wrongdoing that causes spiritual death.

**Mosque:** A Muslim house of worship.

**Muslim:** A follower of the Islamic religion.

**Mysticism:** Religion based on intense spiritual experiences.

## N

**Natural history:** An ancient and medieval term for the study of nature.

**New Testament:** The second part of the Bible, the Christian holy book.

**New World:** The European term for the Americas.

**Nobility:** Members of the upper social class.

**Novella:** A form of short fictitious story originating in Italy.

**Nun:** A woman who is a member of a religious order and lives in a convent.

## O

**Occult:** An aspect of religion that relies on magic and mythology.

**Old Testament:** The first part of the Bible, the Christian holy book.

**Opera:** A musical work that combines choruses in complex harmony, solo ensembles, arias, dances, and independent instrumental pieces.

**Oratorio:** A lengthy religious choral work that features singing that resembles speaking in the form of arias and choruses without action or scenery.

**Oratory:** Public speaking.

**Orbit:** The path of a heavenly body such as a planet.

**P**

**Pagan:** A person who has no religious beliefs or worships more than one god.

**Papacy:** The office of the pope.

**Papal:** Relating to a pope or the Roman Catholic Church.

**Papal State:** The territory owned by the Roman Catholic Church and governed by the pope.

**Parish:** A local church community.

**Parliament:** The main governing body of Britain.

**Patron:** A financial supporter.

**Peace of Westphalia (1648):** An agreement that ended the Thirty Years' War; by it, Catholic and Protestant states were given equal status within the Holy Roman Empire.

**Penance:** An act performed to seek forgiveness of sins.

**Persecution:** Harassment for religious beliefs.

**Philosophy:** The search for a general understanding of values and reality through speculative thinking.

**Physics:** The science that deals with energy and matter and their interactions.

**Piety:** Dutifulness in religion.

**Pilgrimage:** A religious journey.

**Plague:** A widespread communicable disease.

**Planetary motion:** The movement of planets around the Sun.

**Pope:** The supreme head of the Roman Catholic Church.

**Predestination:** The belief that the fate of all humans is determined by a divine force.

**Prince:** A political and military leader; Renaissance ruler.

**Prior:** The head of a monastery.

**Protestantism:** Christian religion established by reformers who separated from the Roman Catholic Church.

**Protestant Reformation:** The reform movement that established a Christian religion separate from the Roman Catholic Church.

**Purgatory:** A place between heaven and hell.

## Q

**Quadrant:** A device in the shape of a quarter circle that measures angles up to 90 degrees and is used for determining altitudes.

**Quest:** A religious journey.

## R

**Regent:** One who rules in place of a minor or an absent monarch.

**Relief:** A carving or sculpture with detail raised above the surface.

**Renaissance:** The transition period in European history from medieval to modern times, marked by a revival of classical culture, which brought innovations in the arts and literature and initiated modern science.

**Rhetoric:** Art of effective speaking and writing.

**Roman Catholic Church:** Christian religion based in Rome, Italy, and headed by a pope.

## S

**Sack of Rome (1527):** Destruction of parts of Rome by armies of Emperor Charles V.

**Sacraments:** Rites of the Catholic Church: communion, baptism, confirmation, penance, anointing of the sick, marriage, and holy offices.

**Sacrilege:** The violation of anything considered sacred to God.

**Saint:** A person who is declared holy by the Catholic Church.

**Salic law:** A law stating that a male could be the only legitimate heir to the throne.

**Salon:** A gathering of nobles for discussion of literature and ideas.

**Salvation:** The forgiveness of sins.

## W

**War of the Roses (1455–85):** Conflict between the houses of York and Lancaster in England that resulted in the founding of the House of Tudor.

**West Roman Empire:** Countries of western Europe; based in Rome, Italy, and formed after the split of the Roman Empire in A.D. 395.

**Witchcraft:** The practice of communicating with supernatural spirits to bring about certain events or results.

## Y

**Year of Jubilee:** A special spiritual celebration held every twenty-five years by the Catholic Church.

# Isaac Abrabanel

**1437
Lisbon, Portugal
1508
Venice, Italy**

**Court official, scholar**

Isaac Abrabanel (also spelled Abravanel) was a Portuguese-Jewish court official and scholar who contributed to the study of biblical texts during the Renaissance. The Renaissance was a cultural movement initiated by scholars called humanist, who promoted the revival of the human-centered literature and philosophy of ancient Greece and Rome as well as new translations of biblical texts (Hebrew holy books and the Christian Bible). His significance to both Jewish history and the Renaissance period can best be understood in the context of events in Spain and Portugal during the fifteenth century.

Abrabanel was born in Lisbon, Portugal, into a distinguished Jewish family. As a youth he received an extensive education in the Talmud (Jewish laws), rabbinic (Jewish theological) literatures, and ancient Greek works. Known for his keen intellect and business ability, he attracted the attention of King Afonso V (1432–1481; ruled 1438–81) of Portugal. Afonso appointed Abrabanel treasurer of the royal court, a position he held until 1481. Abrabanel's presence at court caused a public sensation. People were shocked that a Catholic ruler would give such a high office to a Jew. The

"Let me make this matter perfectly clear to all present: I will not allow the voice of Israel to be stilled on this day."

*Isaac Abrabanel quoted in Gates of Jewish Heritage. [Online] Available http://www.jewishgates.org/personalities/2abrav.stm, April 5, 2002.*

"court Jew" was not a new phenomenon, since Jews were becoming increasingly powerful in courts throughout Europe (see accompanying box). They were invaluable to rulers not only for their administrative expertise but also for their wealth, which helped monarchs wage wars and prop up sagging economies. Nevertheless, at that time on the Iberian Peninsula (the area occupied by Spain and Portugal) relations between Christians and Jews were extremely tense.

## Jews targeted by Christians

The roots of these tensions dated back at least eleven centuries. Jews had arrived on the peninsula around A.D. 300, becoming both urban and rural dwellers. Christians immediately began pressuring Jews to convert to Christianity. The Jews therefore welcomed an invasion of the Moors in 711. (Moors were Muslim Arabs and Berbers from North Africa; Muslims are followers of the Islam religion.) The Muslim conquest was economically attractive to Jews, since it opened the markets of North Africa and the entire Muslim world as far away as India. Jews became highly influential during the tenth through the twelfth centuries, a period that is often called the "Golden Age" of Jewish history. During this time Jews not only produced great works of philosophy, poetry, liturgy (texts for worship services), theology (philosophy of religion), and literature, but they also served as the vital intellectual link between the Muslim Middle East and Christian Europe.

Eventually feuds and dynastic (ruling family) disputes arose among the Muslims on the Iberian Peninsula. In the eleventh century Christian states in the north of Spain, even though they were not unified, took advantage of Muslim unrest and set out to recapture territories conquered by the Moors. The Moors surrendered Toledo to the Christians in 1085. This was a disastrous development for Jews, who once again had to deal with discrimination under Christians. In 1233 Pope Gregory IX (before 1170–1241; reigned 1227–41) established the Inquisition (now known as the medieval Inquisition). This official church court was charged with finding and punishing pagans and heretics (those who did not adhere to the laws of the Catholic Church), namely Jews and Muslims, in Europe.

**Court Jews**

During the Renaissance many Jewish merchants and traders served on the courts of European rulers. Through their connections with Jewish traders in the Ottoman Empire, European Jews were ideally suited to supply armies with grain, timber, horses, and cattle. They also supplied rulers with diamonds, precious stones, and other luxury items. Jews were valued for their organizational skills. Rulers turned to individual Jews who were able to offer reliable, speedy, and extensive supplies of foodstuffs, cloth, and weapons for the army, the central instrument of the prince's power. Court Jews were often employed as tax administrators and court minters (those who made coins), and they engaged in secret and delicate diplomatic efforts on a ruler's behalf. Forming strong personal bonds with the ruler, court Jews were entrusted with arranging transfers of credit and providing assistance to the ruler.

Court Jews were especially prominent in the states of the Holy Roman Empire following the Thirty Years' War (1618-48), a conflict that involved all the major powers of Europe. The war had left the Holy Roman Empire seriously weakened, and rulers within the empire needed people who were loyal to them. Jews with extensive trading and political connections were attractive figures. Some rose to positions of unique influence and affluence and were regarded as indispensable by their ruler. A typical example was Samuel Oppenheimer (c. 1630–1703), who served under Holy Roman Emperor Leopold I (1640–1705; ruled 1658–1705), a member of the Habsburg dynasty based in Austria. In the early 1670s, only a few years after Leopold had expelled more than three thousand Jews from Vienna, Oppenheimer was called back to Vienna to help supply the Habsburg army. Awarded the title of imperial military factor, Oppenheimer developed an extensive operation that included many agents, contractors, and subcontractors throughout the empire and beyond. These connections enabled him to provide substantial supplies and foodstuffs to the Austrian armies and huge sums of money to the emperor. He also engaged in diplomatic activity on the emperor's behalf. Oppenheimer's activity, like that of some other court Jews, was performed in the face of adversity, as various forces within the Habsburg court plotted against him and tried to curtail his power.

During the Inquisition thousands of non-Christians were killed by mobs, while thousands more tried to save their own lives by converting to Christianity. Some Jews, called Marranos (also Conversos), pretended to convert to Christianity while continuing to still secretly practice Judaism (the Jewish religion). "Converted" Muslims who still practiced Islam

An engraving depicting a trial during the Spanish Inquisition. *Reproduced by permission of Fortean Picture Library.*

were called Moriscos. Religious fanaticism soon intensified. For a time Jews' property was seized, but they did not receive any further punishment. The situation changed after 1474, however. At that time Pope Sixtus IV (1414–1484; reigned 1471–84) gave Spanish monarchs Ferdinand II (1452–1516) of Aragon and Isabella I (1451–1504) of Castile—called the Catholic Sovereigns—permission to conduct the Spanish Inquisition, which was to be separate from the medieval Inquisition.

## Spanish monarchs expand Inquisition

The marriage of Ferdinand and Isabella had united Aragon and Castile, large provinces in Spain. The monarchs now wanted to bring the remainder of the Iberian Peninsula under their control. To do this they had to crush opposition groups, centralize the government, and unify the Spanish kingdoms. Their most controversial actions involved Jews and Muslims. Isabella believed that only Catholicism could unite the separate provinces of Spain. In 1474 the king and queen started the Spanish Inquisition to enforce Catholicism as the sole religion of Spain. Their adviser was Tomás de Torquemada (pronounced tor-kay-MAH-thah; 1420–1498), a Dominican monk (member of a religious order founded by Saint Dominic). In 1487 Torquemada was promoted to grand inquisitor (supreme head of the court), and he set out to rid Spain of "converts" who did not actually practice Christianity. Those who did not confess their sins or undergo genuine conversion were severely punished or executed. Practicing Jews were segregated and forced to wear an identifying badge.

The campaign to drive out non-Christians reached a peak in 1492, when Ferdinand and Isabella conquered the Muslim-held Spanish province of Granada. On March 30,

1492, the king and queen issued the Edict of Expulsion, ordering all Jews to leave Spanish territory by July 30. Those who chose to stay in Spain had to submit to baptism (a ceremony marking admission into the Christian religion) or be put to death. Jews were forbidden to take most of their possessions with them if they chose to leave the country. Expelled Jews went mainly to North Africa. About one hundred thousand fled to Portugal, but they soon had to leave because Portugal had entered an alliance with Spain.

## Abrabanel resists expulsion

Abrabanel was serving at Afonso's court during the Spanish Inquisition. A Portuguese Inquisition was not started until 1536, so no official measures were taken against Jews in Portugal during his lifetime. After Afonso died in 1481, however, Abrabanel came under suspicion of conspiring with Afonso's grandson, Ferdinand, duke of Braganza, against the new Portuguese king, John II (1455–1495; ruled 1481–95). Ferdinand was executed in 1483, and Abrabanel barely escaped death by fleeing to Castile. In 1484, despite the Inquisition, he was appointed minister of state at the court of Ferdinand and Isabella. Along with the court rabbi Abraham Senior (see accompanying box) he gave not only administrative service but also a substantial amount of his own money to the king and queen. Abrabanel remained at the Spanish court until 1492, when the monarchs issued the Edict of Expulsion. An unconverted Jew, Abrabanel vigorously resisted being expelled from the country. He vainly tried to have the order revoked. As part of a final effort Abrabanel made a formal response to Ferdinand and Isabella, which he claimed to deliver on behalf of Abraham Senior and other Jewish leaders. In his opening statement quoted from *Gates of Jewish Heritage,* he described the Jews as harmless people who were being mistreated by the king and queen:

An engraving of Jews being expelled from Spain in 1492 by command of the Spanish monarchs Ferdinand and Isabella. *©Bettmann/Corbis. Reproduced by permission of Corbis Corporation.*

Your Majesties, Abraham Senior and I thank you for this opportunity to make our last statement on the behalf of the Jewish communities that we represent..... it is no great honor when a Jew is asked to plead for the safety of his people.

But it is a greater disgrace when the King and Queen of Castile and Aragon, indeed of all Spain, have to seek their glory in the expulsion of a harmless people.

I find it very difficult to understand how every Jewish man, woman, and child can be a threat to the Catholic faith. Very, very strong charges.

We destroy you?

It is indeed the opposite. Did you not admit in this edict to having confined all Jews to restricted quarters and to having limited our legal and social privileges, not to mention forcing us to wear shameful badges? Did you not tax us oppressively? Did you not terrorize us day and night with your diabolical Inquisition? Let me make this matter perfectly clear to all present: I will not allow the voice of Israel to be stilled on this day.

## Influenced by humanism

Abrabanel's resistance was unsuccessful, and he finally chose to flee to Italy rather than convert to Christianity. He spent his remaining years in various centers in Italy, primarily Naples, Monopoli, and Venice. During this time he worked at the courts of Naples and Venice. He also composed most of his works, a combination of commentaries on the Hebrew Bible (the Old Testament in the Christian Bible) and theological studies. Together they formed one of the largest and most diverse Hebrew literary collections of medieval or Renaissance times. The teachings, methods, and sources of Abrabanel's writings reflected Jewish scholarship of the late Middle Ages. Yet his works also addressed many Renaissance themes, such as humanist methods and intellectual concerns. Humanism was a movement that promoted the revival of ancient Greek and Roman culture, especially philosophical and literary texts, as well as the works of early Christian fathers. Humanists were instrumental in initiating the Renaissance, which started in Florence, Italy, in the mid-1300s and began spreading to the rest of Europe in the fifteenth century.

Abrabanel had been exposed to humanism at the court of Afonso V. While living in Castile, Abrabanel spent much of his time in the service of the house (noble family) of

## Abraham Senior

Abraham Senior (born 1412) served with Isaac Abrabanel on the court of Spanish monarchs Ferdinand and Isabella. He was named court rabbi in 1476, most likely as a reward for arranging Ferdinand's marriage to Isabella. Their marriage resulted in the unification of Aragon and Castile, two large Spanish provinces. Abraham's appointment was protested by some in the Jewish community who charged that he did not have the qualifications to be a rabbi. Not only did he lack a scholarly background, they said, but he also did not observe Jewish traditions. Many Jews called him "Sonei Or" (Enemy of Light). Nevertheless, the king and queen continued to give him preferential treatment. In 1488 they appointed him treasurer-general of Santa Hermandad, a national militia (citizens army), which they used to put down revolts. Abraham had full control of all of Santa Hermandad's funds. One reason Abraham was given so much power was that, like Isaac Abrabanel, he provided a considerable amount of his own money to Ferdinand and Isabella.

In 1492 Abrabanel issued a blistering response to the Edict of Expulsion, noting that he spoke on behalf of Abraham Senior and other Jews. Yet historians are not certain how Abraham Senior reacted to the edict. According to unsubstantiated reports, he tried to negotiate with the king to prevent Jews from being expelled. It is a fact, however, that both Abraham Senior and his son-in-law Meir Melamed, the court tax collector and rabbi (he replaced Abraham), were pressured to convert to Christianity. Abraham was severely criticized by most Jews for this act, but he may have been responding to Isabella's threat that if he and Melamed were not baptized, all the Jewish communities would be destroyed. Abraham Senior and Melamed were apparently not the only Jews to give in to such demands. After the Edict of Expulsion, the entire administration of Aragon was headed by converted Jews.

Mendoza. Among his employers was Cardinal Pedro González de Mendoza (1428–1495), a leading sponsor of Renaissance scholarship and architecture in Castile. In 1483 and 1484 Abrabanel wrote commentaries on the biblical books of Joshua, Judges, and 1 and 2 Samuel. These works reveal that he was interested in questions pertaining to the authors of scripture (text of the Bible), the dates when the texts were written, and the origins of biblical books. Abrabanel was following the new humanist methodology, which stressed analysis of the historical and social background of a literary work. Historians note that Abrabanel may have been the first scholar outside of Italy to apply Renaissance concepts to Hebrew literature.

After the 1492 expulsion Abrabanel spent two years in Naples, a major Renaissance center, where he presumably met many influential people. Among them was Giovanni Pontano (1426–1503), head of the renowned humanist academy in Naples. Pontano was a senior member of the upper levels of the Neapolitan court, into which Abrabanel was quickly inducted. Also residing in Naples at this time was Judah Messer Leon, foremost among a number of Jewish-Italian scholars who were receptive to Renaissance trends. Abrabanel's early Italian Renaissance learning, however, was apparently most indebted to Yohanan Alemanno (c. 1435–c. 1504), a Jewish colleague of the celebrated Florentine humanist Giovanni Pico della Mirandola (called Pico; 1463–1494). Historians suggest that although Abrabanel did not mention Alemanno in his writings, he most certainly encountered Alemanno's teachings in Pico's works. Abrabanel may also have had connection through his eldest son, Judah Abrabanel (known as Leone Ebreo; c. 1460–1521). Judah was the author of *Dialoghi di amore* (Dialogues on Love), a famous Renaissance work that was used by the Italian writer **Baldasarre Castiglione** (see entry) in *Book of the Courtier*.

Alemanno developed a philosophical system based on Islamic and Jewish medieval traditions, as well as the fifteenth-century humanists in Florence. According to Alemanno, love of God is the main factor that allows humans to return to their origin, the divine creator. The best model for this journey, he said, can be found in the Song of Songs (the book of Solomon) in the Bible. In the introduction to *Heshek Shlomo,* Alemanno described the perfection of King Solomon, the alleged author of the Song of Songs, who was a universal sage (wise man) according to humanist standards. Alemanno addressed Jews of his own time, pointing out that the doctrines humanists were trying to retrace in the Bible and other ancient texts actually were derived from God's revelation to Abraham, Moses, the Hebrew prophets, and all the people of Israel.

Abrabanel's familiarity with the Renaissance themes adopted by Alemanno appears in his commentaries on the biblical books 1 and 2 Kings, which he completed a year after his arrival in Italy. In later Italian works both Isaac and Judah

Abrabanel expressed other Italian Renaissance concepts, such as a Jewish version of Pico's *prisca theologia* (ancient theology). According to Pico, it is possible to discover a single truth underlying the diverse works written in ancient times. Abrabanel also denied Christian claims of Jesus Christ as the Messiah (savior of the world), which was a dangerous position to take at that time. Abrabanel's works were read later in the sixteenth century by both Jewish and Christian scholars.

## For More Information

### Books

Netanyahu, B. *Don Isaac Abrabanel: Statesman and Philosopher,* fifth edition, Ithaca, N.Y.: Cornell University Press, 1999.

### Web Sites

Knight, Kevin. "Don Isaac Abrabanel." *Catholic Encyclopedia.* [Online] Available http://www.newadvent.org/cathen/01050b.htm, April 4, 2002.

Lipman, David E. "Abraham Senior." *Gates of Jewish Heritage.* [Online] Available http://www.jewishgates.org/personalities/2senior.stm, April 4, 2002.

Lipman, David E. "Isaac ben Judah Abrabanel." *Gates of Jewish Heritage.* [Online] Available http://www.jewishgates.org/personalities/2abrav.stm, April 4, 2002.

# Alexander VI

**January 1, 1431**
**Játiva, Spain**
**August 18, 1503**
**Rome, Italy**

**Pope**

Alexander VI was pope (supreme head of the Roman Catholic Church) from 1492 to 1503 and stands as one of the most controversial of all Renaissance popes. He has been widely condemned for disregarding the priestly vows of celibacy (not engaging in sexual relations) and placing his political goals above spiritual leadership. He shocked his contemporaries by openly acknowledging his illegitimate (born out of wedlock) children. Alexander practiced simony, or selling church offices, and was notorious for his nepotism (favoritism based on kinship). He used his power as pope to enrich his children, he supported a mob of Spanish relatives in Rome, and he created positions for nineteen Spanish cardinals. Although many of the tales about Alexander's corrupt activities have been discounted by historians, he remains a notorious figure in the popular imagination.

## Encounters success and mistrust

Alexander VI was born Rodrigo Borja in Játiva, Spain. Both his father and mother were members of the Borja fami-

*Alexander VI. Photograph courtesy of The Library of Congress.*

10

ly, perhaps the most notorious family of Renaissance Italy. He studied at the University of Valencia and later, in the early 1450s, worked toward a degree in canon (church) law at the University of Bologna. His uncle Alonso was bishop of Valencia and a cardinal. Rodrigo had been preparing for a career within the church since childhood. He first rose to prominence in 1455, when Alonso was elected Pope Calixtus III (1378–1458; reigned 1455–58). Like his uncle, Rodrigo changed his name to Borgia, the Italian form of Borja. When Borgia was twenty-five, his uncle made him a cardinal, and at twenty-six he became vice chancellor of the papal court, a position he held for thirty-five years.

Borgia lived a secular (nonreligious) life in Rome and did not become a priest until 1468, when he was thirty-seven years old. His many connections made him extremely wealthy, and being a priest did not change his life. Handsome and attractive to women, Borgia was intelligent, a good public speaker, and popular with the citizens of Rome. While he was a cardinal he fathered at least seven illegitimate children. Historians are certain about the identity of only one woman, Vanozza de' Catanei (1470–1492), as being the mother of four of his children: Cesare (c. 1475–1507), Juan (1476–1497), Lucrezia (1480–1519), and Jofré (1481–1517). Despite his popularity amongst the general populace, Borgia's colleagues initially mistrusted him. He had little experience outside Rome (except for his service as a legate, or official representative, in Spain from 1472 to 1473), but he was keenly interested in politics. He became a major figure in the college of cardinals (a committee of cardinals who elect the pope). His immense wealth and political connections allowed him to secure this importance and overcome the doubts of his detractors.

## Becomes Alexander VI

At a meeting of church officials held in August 1492, the sixty-one-year-old Borgia was elected pope. He took the name of Alexander VI in honor of the ancient emperor Alexander the Great. His reign began well. The people were pleased by his election, and he began extensive building projects, working diligently at papal business. Trouble began in 1494, however, after the death of King Ferdinand I of Naples (1423–1494; ruled 1458–94). The Kingdom of Naples had once been a possession of the French throne, and King Charles VIII of France (1470–1498; ruled 1483–98) decided to reclaim it. He invaded Italy and reached Rome in December 1494, thus starting the Italian Wars (1494–1559), a conflict between France and Spain over control of Italy. Alexander feared that he would be removed from his position by the French, but he managed to negotiate his freedom. He then joined forces with Germany, Spain, Milan, and Venice and expelled Charles from Italy.

Considerable opposition to Alexander among the cardinals began during the French campaign in Italy. Many felt that Alexander was driven more by a desire to increase his family's importance and wealth rather than to promote the welfare of the Catholic Church. During the conquest of Naples it seemed that Alexander exploited the vulnerable position of King Alfonso II of Naples (1449–1496; ruled 1494–95), trading Vatican support in order to gain land, titles, and marriage partners for some of his children. Nevertheless, Alexander was credited with keeping the French out of Italy. He was also praised for his handling of negotiations with Charles when the king passed through Rome in December 1494 and January 1495. Meanwhile, Alexander faced the monumental task of regaining control of the Papal States (territories in Italy under the direct control of the pope), which had fallen into the hands of local nobles during the reign of his predecessor, Innocent VIII (1432–1492; reigned 1484–92). Alexander delegated this task to his son Cesare Borgia, who accomplished it with brutal determination.

In 1499 Cesare's marriage to the French princess Charlotte d'Albret forced Alexander into a very unwise course of action. The marriage committed Alexander to friendship with the new French king, Louis XII (1462–1515; ruled 1498–1515). In exchange for French help in once again conquering the Papal States, Alexander did not interfere with Louis's conquest of Milan and granted the king an annulment (an order that declares a marriage invalid) of his marriage. In this way Alexander betrayed his countrymen and reversed his anti-French policy.

Cesare Borgia's duchy of Romagna was the most substantial of the endowments Alexander gave to his children. He arranged for his daughter Lucrezia to marry Alfonso d'Este (1486–1534) after her two previous husbands had been disposed of when they no longer suited Alexander's plans. The marriage was intended to provide support for Cesare from Ferrara. Lucrezia and other Borgia children (including Giovanni, the son of one of Alexander's mistresses) were given lands taken from leading Roman baronial families. By the end of Alexander's reign, most of the barons were in exile (forced absence from the country) and their lands were in the possession of the Borgias. Though the barons soon recovered their land after the pope's death. Again, some historians have argued that Alexander intended to impose order and increase the authority of the papacy. At the time, however, many church officials considered Alexander an opportunist who was more interested in family matters than in church policies.

## Confronts Savonarola

One of Alexander's harshest critics was Girolamo Savonarola (pronounced sah-voh-nah-RO-lah; 1452–1498), head of the monastery of San Marco in Florence and an advocate of church reform. Angered by the corrupt behavior of church officials, Savonarola demanded stricter adherence to the spiritual values and greater awareness of the poor. Savonarola was also known for his visions, with which he claimed to predict the future. Earning the title of the "Preacher of the Despairing," Savonarola gave immensely popular sermons. His sermons reached a peak during Advent (the period beginning the four Sundays preceding Christmas) in 1492, when Alexander became the new pope. Savonarola prophesied the coming of the "Scourge [whip] of Italy," a vision that may have been prompted by Alexander's controversial behavior. Determined to reform the church in Florence, Savonarola formed his own congregation, which was soon expanded to include monasteries (houses for monks, members of a religious order) in other parts of Italy. He had also been criticizing the Florence city government. In 1494 Savonarola's prophecy of the "Scourge of Italy" was fulfilled when Charles VIII invaded Italy. Piero de' Medici (1471–1503), duke of Florence, fled from Italy and threw himself upon the mercy of the French king. The Signoria (ruling body of Florence) elected Savonarola to ask Charles to protect Florence. Savonarola then turned to the problem of a new government without the Medicis. In 1495 he was opposed by a group of priests, nuns, and monks called the *Tie-*

# Reformation Popes

The reign of Pope Alexander VI came to symbolize the corruption of the Roman Catholic Church. During Alexander's reign, critics such as the Florentine monk Girolamo Savonarola began calling for reform and a renewed commitment to Christian values. Within twenty years after Savonarola's death, the rapid rise of Protestantism brought more demands for reform. In keeping with a practice dating back to early times, many religious and political leaders wanted to hold a general council of bishops to discuss problems. The council met at Rome from 1515 until 1517. This gathering, called the Fifth Lateran Council, agreed to make various reforms.

Popes showed no serious interest in reform until 1537, when Pope Paul III (1468–1549; reigned 1534–49) appointed a committee of cardinals to study problems in the church. It adjourned shortly before the German reformer Martin Luther posted his Ninety-Five Theses, a list of criticisms of the church, at Wittenberg, Germany, in 1517. Their report, *A Council ... for Reforming the Church,* denounced evils and abuses at all levels. Most of these abuses were laid at the door of the papacy itself. The report was part of the first stage of the movement called the Catholic Reformation (also known as the Counter Reformation). For the next few years Pope Paul tried to convene a council, but it had to be postponed several times. In the meantime he initiated his own reforms. He encouraged many new religious communities and approved the Society of Jesus (Jesuits) for men in 1540 and the Order of Saint Ursula for women in 1544. In 1542 he founded the

*pidi* (the lukewarm), who objected to his strict reforms. The Tiepidi received support from the Holy League, which needed backing from Florence. But first they had to remove Savonarola from power.

In 1495 Alexander sent a letter to Savonarola stating that he had been accused of heresy (violation of church laws), false prophecy, and troubling the peace of the church. Alexander summoned Savonarola to Rome. Savonarola was ill at the time, so the pope let him stay in Florence on the condition that he stop preaching. In 1496 the people of Florence persuaded Alexander to allow Savonarola to preach Lenten sermons. By that time city leaders were distancing themselves from him, and in 1497 the Signoria began limiting his preaching. When a riot took place during one of Savonarola's

Congregation of the Roman Inquisition as the final court of appeal in trials of heresy.

The first session of a council of bishops finally met at Trent in northern Italy in 1545. Called the Council of Trent, the group clarified and affirmed many practices of the church, mostly in response to the charges of Protestant reformer Martin Luther (1483–1546). The second session met at Trent in 1551 and 1552 under Pope Julius III (1487–1555; reigned 1550–55), and the participants clarified more church doctrines. The next pope, Paul IV (1476–1559; reigned 1555–59), opposed the council as a threat to papal authority, so he started his own reform measures. In 1555 he strengthened the Roman Inquisition. At that time the Roman Catholic Church wrongly suspected Jews of influencing the Protestant Reformation, so the pope established the Jewish ghetto (a part of the city in which a minority group is forced to live) in Rome. He also required all Jews to wear an identifying badge, thus separating them from Christians. In 1559 Paul IV issued the first edition of his Index of Prohibited Books, a list of works that the church considered to be heretical. It was used in conjunction with the Inquisition to stop the flow of heretical ideas. The next pope, Pius V (1504–1572; reigned 1566–72), was not so brutal as Paul IV, but he was determined to suppress heresy and all other violations of church laws. In fact, Pius V himself took part in many Inquisition proceedings. During his reign, Protestantism was completely eliminated in Italy.

sermons, Florentine leaders identified him as the source of discontent in the city. Alexander then excommunicated (forced to officially leave the church) Savonarola and his followers for heresy. The final showdown between Alexander and Savonarola began in February 1498, when Alexander ordered the Signoria to silence the disobedient monk. In April, Florentine officials put Savonarola on trial, then a church trial took place in May. Savonarola and two of his followers were convicted of heresy and executed by hanging.

## A pope to be feared—and respected

Alexander was infamous throughout Europe, but he was especially unpopular in Rome. One reason was that he was a Spanish pope in a court increasingly dominated by Italians. But the main reason was that people genuinely feared him. He threatened those who crossed him, and suspicious deaths were linked to him. Even some cardinals did not feel safe in Rome and went into exile. In Alexander's favor, however, it must be said that his morals were no worse than those of his contemporaries and he sincerely loved his family. For instance, he was devastated with grief when his son Giovanni was mysteriously murdered. Although Alexander used his daughter Lucrezia as a political pawn in her three marriages, he could hardly bear to be separated from her. He was frequently maligned (spoken ill of) and satirized (criticized through irony) in his own day, but the most vicious rumors (that he poisoned his enemies, for example) are unfounded.

Despite the fears and uncertainties about his character, Alexander was a cultivated man. As head of the church, his act of most lasting significance was his division of newly discovered lands between Spain and Portugal in the Treaty of Tordesillas (1493). He also encouraged the University of Rome and supported artistic projects. In the Vatican he had the Borgia apartments decorated by the Italian painter Pinturicchio (Betto di Biago; c. 1454–1513). He had an elevated corridor built, linking the Vatican with the papal fortress Castel Sant'Angelo. He had the castle strengthened by the architect Antonio da Sangallo the Elder (1455–1535) and decorated by Pinturcchio. He also commissioned work on several churches in Rome and on fortresses in the Papal States, notably at Civita Castellana. Alexander VI died in 1503, perhaps of malaria (a disease transmitted by the bite of mosquitoes) or complications from fever. He was not killed, as was rumored, by poison prepared for a rich cardinal.

## For More Information

### Books

Bellonci, Maria. *The Life and Times of Lucrezia Borgia,* translated by Bernard and Barbara Wall. London: Phoenix Press, 2000.

Erlanger, Rachel. *Unarmed prophet: Savonarola in Florence.* New York: McGraw-Hill, 1987.

Puzo, Mario. *The Family: A Novel,* completed by Carol Gino. New York: Regan Books, 2001.

## Web Sites

"Alexander VI." *Encyclopedia.com.* [Online] Available http://www.encyclo pedia.com/html/a/alexand6.asp, April 4, 2002.

Knight, Kevin. "Alexander VI." *Catholic Encyclopedia.* [Online] Available http://www.newadvent.org/cathen/01289a.htm, April 4, 2002.

# Sofonisba Anguissola

**1532**
**Cremona, Italy**
**1625**
**Palermo, Italy**

**Painter**

Italian painter Sofonisba Anguissola (pronounced ahn-GWEE-so-lah) was the first woman artist to establish an international reputation and to produce a substantial body of work. Her portraits depicted stories, a technique that was ahead of her time. At the end of the sixteenth century the main interests of Italian art were nature scenes and genre scenes such as the Crucifixion (execution of Jesus Christ on a cross), the Resurrection (Jesus's rising from the dead), and still life. Anguissola inspired other Italian women to take up painting. Among them were Irene di Spilimbergo (1541–1559) and Lavinia Fontana (1552–1614). Spilimbergo took lessons from the Italian master Titian (c. 1488–1576) and produced several paintings. Fontana established a successful career, becoming the first woman artist to receive large public commissions (see accompanying box).

## Specializes in portraits

Born in Cremona, Italy, in 1532, Anguissola was the eldest child in a family of six daughters and a son. She and

**Lavinia Fontana**

Lavinia Fontana was a successful Renaissance woman artist. Like Sofonisba Anguissola, Fontana gained fame as a painter and made a living from her career. She was born in Bologna, Italy, where she studied painting with her father, Prospero Fontana, a well-known artist and teacher. By the age of eighteen she had earned a reputation as a painter of portraits and religious subjects. While working in her father's studio she met fellow painter Giano Paolo Zappi, whom she married in 1577. Zappi apparently gave up his own career to support Fontana's work. He managed the income from her numerous commissions and helped take care of their eleven children.

Fontana was famous for her portraits, including *Self-Portrait at Spinnet* (1577). One of her best-known works is *Portrait of a Noblewoman* (1580), which depicts a young woman standing and caressing a small dog. The portrait shows the artist's skill in giving a sense of realism to the delicate silk underdress that the woman wears beneath an ornately embroidered velvet overdress. Fontana also captured the fine details of the woman's gold, pearl, and ruby jewelry. During the 1590s Fontana focused on religious themes, and she painted several large altarpieces (artwork that is part of the altar, or center of worship, in a church). This was unusual for a woman artist, since women were generally not hired to work on altarpieces. The main reason for this was that women were not allowed to study anatomy or draw nude male models, which was necessary to depict the human figures that were featured in Renaissance religious paintings. Fontana's altarpieces included the *Holy Family with the Sleeping Christ* for the Escorial palace, the famous monastery and royal residence that King Philip II commissioned to be built in Spain. Around 1603, at the invitation of Pope Clement VIII, Fontana moved to Rome as an official painter to the papal court. She painted the altarpiece *The Stoning of St. Stephen Martyr* for the church of San Paolo fuori le Mura. This was her best-known public commission. Fontana's fame continued to grow as her workshops in Rome and Bologna produced works of high quality. Art historians estimate that Fontana produced more than one hundred paintings. Only thirty-two identified as her work have survived, while a small number of others appear to be in her style. Though they are still the largest number of known works created by a woman artist prior to 1700.

her sisters received a humanist education. (Known as *studia humanitatis,* or humanist studies, this was a new curriculum based on ancient Greek and Roman languages and literature. The emphasis on humanist studies initiated the Renaissance.) Four of the Anguissola daughters—Sofonisba, Lucia, Europa, and Anna Maria—became artists, and another, Minerva, was noted for literary studies. Sofonisba's Anguissola emergence as a painter was unusual in a period when women artists were typically trained by their fathers.

Anguissola studied painting with local artists, then she taught her younger sisters. Lucia showed the most interest in art. Anguissola's specialization in portraits and self portraits was shaped by the restraints placed on female artists at the time. They were not allowed to study anatomy or draw male models, which prevented them from creating large-scale historical paintings that featured human forms. Anguissola therefore turned to portraiture. Her depiction of firmly drawn, animated faces within a delicate surrounding was her trademark style. Her earliest known works are the *Portrait of a Nun* (1515) and *Self-Portrait* (1554).

Anguissola's paintings were admired by contemporaries such as the Roman nobleman Tommaso Cavalieri, who disregarded the popular belief that painting was a masculine art. She was encouraged by the great painter **Michelangelo** (1475–1564; see entry). When Michelangelo saw Anguissola's drawing of a smiling girl teaching her nurse to read, he said that a weeping boy would have been more difficult to draw. This comment caused her to draw a boy (her brother Asdrubale) bitten by a crayfish. Anguissola's drawing was probably the model for Carvaggio's painting *Boy Bitten by Lizard* (c. 1596), thus showing her influence on the important artists of her time.

## Serves as court painter

Portrait painting did not receive much respect in the sixteenth century, but Anguissola used it as a way to represent artistic achievement. In *The Chess Game* (1555), she depicted her sisters Lucia, Europa, and Minerva at the chess board. This was meant to demonstrate female excellence at an intellectual game. The painting also hinted at the sisters' shared history as aspiring artists who competed with and learned from one another. In her works of the late 1550s, such as *Bernardino Campi Painting Sofonisba Anguissola* and *The Family Group,* the expression of pride in female achievement is reversed to become a commentary on the male-dominated society, values, and norms.

Anguissola spent the years 1559 to1573 in Madrid, Spain, as court painter and lady-in-waiting to Queen Isabella of Valois, whom she taught to paint. Anguissola's Spanish paintings are not well documented and have been confused with the works of other painters. Among the few portraits known for sure to be Anguissola's are *Philip II* and *Isabella of Valois* (both painted around 1565). Sofonisba's marriage in 1573 to a Sicilian nobleman, Don Fabrizio de Moncada, ended with her husband's untimely death in 1578 or 1579. Her marriage in 1580 to the Genoese nobleman Orazio Lomellini took her to Genoa, Italy, where she remained for the next four decades and invented a new baroque. (The term used to describe the music, art, literature, and philosophy of the seventeenth century; exuberant, sensuous, expressive, and dynamic style.) Her last years were spent in Palermo, Italy. Anguissola' eyesight began to fail at the end of her life and she was unable to paint. In 1624, a year before her death, the Flemish artist Anthony Van Dyck (1599–1641) visited her and sketched her portrait in his notebooks. He noted that she

Anguissola painted *The Chess Game* in order to demonstrate female excellence at an intellectual game. ©*Ali Meyer/Corbis. Reproduced by permission of Corbis Corporation.*

had a clear memory, told good stories, and gave him advice on his own paintings. Anguissola was an important figure, especially for women, in the tradition of Renaissance art.

## For More Information

### Books

Ferino-Pagden, Sylvia, and Maria Kusche. *Sofonisba Anguissola: a Renaissance Woman.* Washington, D.C.: National Museum of Women in the Arts, 1995.

Perlingieri, Ilya Sandra. *Sofonisba Anguissola: The First Great Woman Artist of the Renaissance.* New York: Rizzoli, 1992.

### Web Sites

*Artist Profiles: Lavinia Fontana.* [Online] Available http://www.nmwa.org/legacy/bios/bfontana.htm, April 4, 2002.

"Sofonisba Anguissola." *A Guide to the Collection of European Art to 1900.* [Online] Available http://www.mfa.org/handbook/portrait.asp?id=195.5&s=6, April 4, 2002.

"Sofonisba Anguissola." *Art Cyclopedia.* [Online] Available http://www.artcyclopedia.com/artists/anguissola_sofonisba.html, April 4, 2002.

# Francis Bacon

**January 22, 1561**
**London, England**
**April 9, 1626**
**London, England**

**Philosopher, statesman, and author**

Francis Bacon made many contributions to the English Renaissance as a philosopher, statesman, and author. His advocacy of "active science" influenced the culture of the English-speaking world. He continued the family tradition of serving the royal court, and was made a nobleman during his career. His written works continue to be important in philosophy and history.

"The sovereignty of man lieth hid in knowledge...."

*Francis Bacon.*

## Pursues political career

Francis Bacon was born in London on January 22, 1561, at York House. He was the second son of Sir Nicholas Bacon (1509–1579) and his second wife, Lady Anne Bacon. Through the families of both parents Francis had important connections with the political and cultural life of Tudor England (the period in history when members of the house, or royal family, of Tudor ruled England; 1485–1603). His father was lord keeper of the great seal under **Queen Elizabeth I** (1503–1633; see entry), and his maternal grandfather had been tutor to King Edward VI (1537–1553; ruled 1547–53).

Francis Bacon.

Bacon entered Trinity College, Cambridge, in 1573 and left in 1575 without earning a degree. The following year he accompanied Amias Paulet (c. 1536–1588), the English ambassador to France. This was Bacon's only trip abroad. He returned to England after the death of his father. Finding himself in difficult financial circumstances, he enrolled at Gray's Inn and became a barrister, or lawyer, in 1582. The previous year he had been elected member of Parliament (the main law-making body of Great Britain) for the Cornish borough of Bossiney, and he served in every parliament thereafter until 1621.

Bacon's public career began with his election to Parliament, where he displayed great talent. Apart from an appointment to the clerkship of the Star Chamber (a meeting place of the English monarch's councilors) in 1589, however, he was not given favor in the court of Elizabeth I. His ambition for high office was frustrated by the efforts of William Cecil (1520–1598), the father of Robert Cecil (1563–1612), who saw Bacon as a competitor for Elizabeth's favor. When Robert succeeded William as the chief minister to **King James I** (1566–1625; see entry) in 1603, he continued efforts to impede Bacon's professional progress. Bacon was determined to further his career, so he attached himself to Robert Devereux (1566–1601), earl of Essex, in 1591. Though he was still unable to secure a position within the government. In 1592, on the anniversary of the Queen's coronation, Essex presented a speech composed by Bacon. In this speech which praised knowledge, Bacon stated his lifelong theme: "the sovereignty of man lieth hid in knowledge ... now we govern nature in opinions, but are thrall to her in necessities; but if we would be led by her in invention, we should command her in action."

When Essex was tried for treason (betrayal of one's country) in 1601 after a failed revolt, Bacon was assigned to prosecute his former patron. The job continued to haunt him years later, so much so that he felt compelled to defend himself in *Apology* in 1604. While his part in the fate of Essex has been criticized as an ungrateful betrayal, it has also been defended as a duty painfully performed.

## Meets with trouble

Bacon was knighted (honored by the monarch for merit) when James took the throne, but it was his appoint-

### Bacon's Political Fall

During the height of his political career, Bacon managed to have his new chief rival, Edward Coke, dismissed as chief justice of the King's Bench in 1616. Despite Bacon's apparent abilities, he was still overshadowed by a royal favorite, this time a man named George Villiers. Villiers was named marquis and subsequently duke of Buckingham by James I. The new duke of Buckingham soon found himself involved in controversy, as royal monopolies (companies that dominate the market to prevent competition) that made their money from indirect taxation had alienated much of the nobility. Coke was elected to Parliament in 1621 and soon led an attack on the monopolies. This move threatened Buckingham's position. To save one of his chief officers, James I reluctantly allowed Coke to charge Bacon rather than Buckingham with bribery and corruption. These charges were essentially unjustified. Bacon had done no more than accept the usual fees of office, and no one could prove that his judgment had been affected by accepting these fees. His fall was dictated by politics. Among the penalties levied on Bacon was forced resignation, a fine of forty thousand pounds, imprisonment in the Tower of London (a prison for members of the royalty and nobility), and a prohibition from serving in Parliament. The fine, imprisonment, and the prohibition from holding office were not enforced, however.

ment as solicitor in 1607 that gave his fortunes the greatest boost. In 1608 he was named treasurer of Gray's Inn, where he maintained lodgings to the end of his life. He was finally appointed attorney general in 1613. Four years later Bacon was given his father's old position, lord keeper of the seal, and he ascended to the highest position in the kingdom, lord chancellor, in 1618. The same year he was also given the title of Baron Verulam, and in 1621 he became Viscount Saint Albans. He had reached the height of his career, only to be brought down by the political manipulations of his new rival, Edward Coke (1552–1634; see accompanying box).

## Writes on new method

Bacon's first publication, in 1597, was a collection of ten essays mainly devoted to aphorisms (concise statements of truth or sentiment) on political behavior. These were expanded and twenty-nine new essays published with them in

1612. A still further enlarged edition, including fifty-eight essays, appeared in 1625. Between 1603, when he was knighted, and 1607, when he was appointed solicitor general, he
published *The Advancement of Learning* (1605) in hopes of
moving James to support science. In 1623 this work was expanded as *De augmentis scienarium* (On the wisdom of science) Bacon published *De sapientia veterum* (On the wisdom
of the ancients), an interpretation of ancient myths, and *The
Beginning of the History of Great Britain* in 1619. The following
year he wrote the *Novum organum* (New method) as Part II of
*The Great Instauration*. The entire project was never completed, and the only existing part is in itself incomplete, but
Bacon's reputation as a philosopher of science rests mainly
upon it. The plan for the renewal of the sciences had six
parts: a survey of existing knowledge, Bacon's inductive logic
(method of arriving at a general conclusion on the basis of
particular facts), an encyclopedia of all natural phenomena,
examples of the new method's application, Bacon's discoveries, and an exposition of the new philosophy that would finally emerge. His new philosophy was based on a critique of
the works of the ancient Greek philosopher Aristotle
(384–322 B.C.) and his followers. Bacon wished to produce a
critical method for achieving knowledge. He divided human
reasoning into two distinct processes or "moments": invention and judgment. He then showed how these two principles
were related, formulating complicated new theories.

Bacon was also interested in educational reform, and
he stressed the practical aspects of science. Despite being a
contemporary of the Italian astronomer **Galileo** (1564–1642;
see entry) and other founders of modern science, he knew little of their achievements. Instead, he based his ideas on classical sources and his contributions to science were limited to
theories he described in his books. Bacon himself did not
make scientific observations or conduct experiments, but he
felt that Aristotle's system was not suited to discovery of new
truth. Bacon also rejected the ideas of the ancient Greek
philosopher Plato (c. 428–c. 348 B.C.) because they turned the
mind inward upon itself, "away from observation and away
from things." Bacon's new method emphasized "the com-
merce of the mind with things." Science was to be experimental, to take note of how human activity produces changes in
things and not merely to record what happens independently

## Petrus Ramus

Scientific method in the Renaissance was also influenced by the French philosopher Petrus Ramus (Pierre de La Ramée; 1515–1572). Ramus was an educational reformer and humanist (scholar who studied ancient literature and languages with an emphasis on human achievement) who reacted against the Aristotelian logic (system of thought based on reason) he had been taught at the University of Paris. Ramus especially wished to revive the mathematical arts of arithmetic, geometry, astronomy, and physics. He wanted to show that they could be put to practical uses. He thought Aristotle's theories on physics were too complicated for educational purposes. Ramus recommended starting with Aristotle's works on mechanical problems and meteorology and biology. He also thought classical texts on mathematics and natural history should be part of the university curriculum. He placed great emphasis on method, but what he meant by this was more a method of teaching than of conducting scientific study.

of what people do. In addition, science should be a practical instrument for human betterment. Bacon's views are best summed up in the section of *Novum organum* titled "The New Philosophy or Active Science": "Man is the helper and interpreter of Nature," he argued. "He can only act and understand insofar as by working upon her he has come to perceive her order. Beyond this he has neither knowledge nor power."

In retirement Bacon produced a great number of other works: expanded editions of the *Essays* (1625) and *The Advancement of Learning,* (1623) *Historia naturalis et experimentalis* (Natural and experimental history; 1622), a collection titled *Apothegms New and Old* (1624), a translation of the Psalms (book of poems in the Bible), and a utopian fable (story about a perfect society featuring animal characters), *The New Atlantis* (1627). Over the centuries many historians have argued that some of the plays attributed to the great Elizabethan playwright **William Shakespeare** (1564–1616; see entry) were actually written by Bacon. Unlike a number of his peers, Bacon's importance was recognized by his contemporaries. His significance to the development of modern science was not so much the specific method he formulated but his arguments against what he called the "idols of the mind," which were popular philosophical and scientific theories of

**The title page from Francis Bacon's *The New Atlantis*.**

the time. He made a lasting contribution with his theory that inquiries should not be made by first principles, or fixed ideas, but instead by first perceptions, and that conclusions should be drawn through progressive stages of observation and experiment.

Bacon spent his last years in bitter retirement, but he was characteristically productive. He attempted to win royal favor again with *History of the Reign of King Henry VII* (1622), now regarded as a classic of Renaissance history. Yet he was unable to gain another royal appointment for even a minor office. In 1606 he married fourteen-year-old Alice Barnham, the heiress of a London alderman. The marriage was childless. In his last months Bacon discovered that Alice was having an affair, so he excluded her from all but her legal portion of his will. He died at Gray's Inn on April 9, 1626.

## For More Information

### Books

Maurier, Daphne du. *The Winding Stair: Francis Bacon, His Rise and Fall.* Garden City, N.Y.: Doubleday, 1977.

### Web Sites

Donnelly, Darri. *The Essays of Francis Bacon.* [Online] Available http://ourworld.compuserve.com/homepages/mike_donnelly/bacon.htm, April 4, 2002.

"Francis Bacon." *The Internet Encyclopedia of Philosophy.* [Online] Available http://www.utm.edu/research/iep/b/bacon.htm, April 4, 2002.

# Pieter Bruegel the Elder

**c. 1525
Breda, Netherlands
1569
Brussels, Belgium**

**Painter, designer**

The Dutch painter and engraving designer Pieter Bruegel (also spelled Brueghel; pronounced BROO-gehl) the Elder is considered one of the foremost artists of the late northern Renaissance. The northern Renaissance was an extension of the Italian Renaissance, a movement based on the revival of ancient Greek and Roman culture (the classical period) that began in Florence, Italy, in the mid-1300s. The Italian Renaissance was initiated by scholars called humanists who promoted the human-centered values of the classical period. Humanist ideals were soon influencing the arts, literature, philosophy, science, religion, and politics in Italy. During the early fifteenth century, innovations of the Italian Renaissance began spreading from Italy into the rest of Europe, where the movement became known as the northern Renaissance. His works provide insight into humans and their relationship with nature. He lived and worked in Antwerp and Brussels (cities in present-day Belgium) at a time when northern European art was strongly influenced by the late Italian Renaissance style called mannerism. Adopted in sculpture as well as painting, mannerism was characterized by distortion of space and elongation of human forms. Although Bruegel used some manner-

**Pieter Bruegel the Elder.**

ist techniques, especially in his later works, he chose to develop his own style by adapting the themes and techniques of earlier artists.

The major source of information concerning Bruegel is the Dutch biographer Karel van Mander (1548–1606), who wrote in 1604. Mander claims that Bruegel was born in a town of the same name near Breda on the present-day Dutch-Belgian border. Most recent authorities, however, follow the Italian writer Francesco Guicciardini (1483–1540) in designating the painter's birthplace as Breda itself. From the fact that Bruegel entered the Antwerp painters' guild in 1551, it is assumed that he was born between 1525 and 1530. His master, or teacher, according to Mander, was the Antwerp painter Pieter Coecke van Aelst (1502–1550). Bruegel married Coecke's daughter, Mayken, in 1563. After studying and working with artists in Antwerp, Bruegel traveled extensively in France, Italy, and the Alps region in the early 1550s. Returning to Antwerp in 1555, he embarked on a successful career. A versatile painter, Bruegel produced landscapes, religious and allegorical subjects (stories with symbolic meaning), scenes of peasant festivities, depictions of Flemish proverbs (brief statements of truth), and compositions in the manner of Hieronymus Bosch (1450–1516; see accompanying box). Bruegel's career falls into two major phases—the first in Antwerp and the second in Brussels.

## Develops his style in Antwerp

In Antwerp, Bruegel produced many designs for the print publisher Hieronymous Cock. His pen drawing titled *Big Fish Eat Little Fish* was published in 1557 as an engraving by Cock. Cock substituted Bosch's name for Bruegel's in order to exploit the fashion for Bosch's works then current in Antwerp. The series *Seven Deadly Sins,* engraved in 1558, carries the artist's own signature, a sign of Bruegel's increasing importance. In these works Bruegel, unlike any of his Antwerp contemporaries, achieved a truly creative synthesis of Bosch's demonic symbolism with his own personal vision of human foolishness and sinfulness.

Bruegel's earliest known paintings were also done in Antwerp. Among them were *Parable of the Sower* (1557), *Chil-*

## Hieronymous Bosch

Hieronymous Bosch (Jheronimus or Jeroen van Aken; 1450–1516) was a Dutch painter who developed a distinctive, often disturbing style. Although Bosch depicted traditional subjects—folk tales, stories about Christ, images of saints—his paintings are filled with bizarre plants and animals, distorted human figures, and amusing cartoon-like creatures. Paying close attention to small details, he used brilliant colors that give a nightmarish, grotesque effect to his pictures. One of his best-known works, *Garden of Earthly Delights,* seems to be an elaborate morality tale (story with a lesson on good and evil) about the punishment of sinners, yet art scholars have not been able to agree on an exact interpretation of the painting. After Bosch died, Pieter Bruegel the Elder and other artists made copies of his paintings and produced new works that imitated his style. Some modern scholars believe Bosch's art was an expression of his disturbed mental state, while others think it was inspired by witchcraft or alchemy (science devoted to turning base metal into gold) and astrology (study of the heavens to predict future events).

dren's Games (1560) and *Combat of Carnival and Lent* (1559). All were inspired by Flemish folk life, but despite their superficial gaiety, they can be interpreted as allegories of a foolish and sinful world. In *Combat of Carnival and Lent,* Bosch's influence is still evident in the landscape with a high horizon (line between Earth and sky), decorative patterns, and many iconographic (symbolic) details. Bruegel's own style can be seen, however, in the use of bright, primary colors and a rhythmic organization of forms. His two most bizarre and illusionistic works are *Dulle Griet* and the *Triumph of Death* (both probably executed in 1562). *Dulle Griet* has features of the Bosch style, but unlike Bosch's works it is not intended so much as a moral sermon against the sinfulness of the world as a recognition of the existence of evil in it. Bruegel's view of evil as being part of the human condition carries over into *Triumph of Death.* This painting has also been interpreted as a reference to the outbreak of religious persecutions in the Netherlands.

The last of Bruegel's Antwerp paintings is the famous *Tower of Babel* (1563). The artist did another version later in Brussels. The image of the Tower of Babel comes from the story in the Book of Genesis in the Bible (the Christian holy book). According to the story, the descendants of Noah, who spoke one language, decided to build a tower that reached heaven in order to gain fame for themselves. As punishment for their excessive pride, they no longer spoke the same language and could not communicate with one another. Thus the tower was never completed. Bruegel intended his painting to symbolize the futility of human ambition, and perhaps more specifically to criticize the spirit of commercialism then reigning in Antwerp.

## Takes new direction in Brussels

In 1563 Bruegel moved to Brussels, where he remained until his death in 1569. Although he had studied in Italy in the early 1550s, he showed little interest in Italian art until this time. Many of his works show closer attention to composition and feature larger-scale figures than visible in Italian art. He was possibly influenced by the Italian painter **Raphael** (1483–1520; see entry). Bruegel reportedly studied cartoons (designs or drawings used as plans for paintings and other works) that Raphael made for works at the Vatican. Bruegel's reputation as one of the greatest of all Netherlandish painters is mainly founded upon the works of the brief but highly productive Brussels period. Beginning this phase was *Road to Calvary* (1564), his largest surviving painting, in which humans are subordinated to the rhythms and patterns of nature. A lower horizon and a new feeling for atmospheric perspective are important stylistic features of this work. In 1565 Bruegel was commissioned to execute a series of pictures of the months for Niclaes Jonghelinck, a wealthy government official. They are based upon the medieval idea of the labors of the seasons. Of the original group, five paintings have survived. Each depicts a two-month period. The central theme of the series is that if humans follow the order of nature, they can avoid the folly for which they are otherwise destined. Bruegel portrayed people as anonymous symbols of humanity who live and work close to the soil in a tranquil state of unity with nature.

The months of December and January are represented by *Hunters in the Snow. Dark Day* depict the labors or February and March, while *Hay Harvest* portray the chores of June and July, respectively. The months of August and September are represented by the golden-hued *Wheat Harvest,* one of the most lyrical panels in the series. Here Bruegel achieved heightened atmospheric effects. The most brilliant panel in the series is *Return of the Herd,* which represents October and November. A magnificent composition, this painting depicts the scope and grandeur of the natural world.

Bruegel addressed a more troubling theme in *Massacre of the Innocents* (c. 1566). Art historians have suggested that it was the artist's criticism of the mounting atrocities of the Spanish Inquisition (a court established by the Roman Catholic Church to find and punish heretics, those who violated the laws of the church) in the Netherlands. In view of Bruegel's deliberate use of the setting of a contemporary Flemish village to stage the events, this view has gained acceptance from most recent authorities. Similar in conception, though differing in spirit, is the *Numbering at Bethlehem* (1566). In this painting, however, Bruegel gave a contemporary interpretation of religious events in order to investigate the varieties of rural life in a winter setting.

## Uses large-figure style

*Peasant Dance* (c. 1566–67) represents a new and important direction that Bruegel was to develop in the last years of his career. In this work the painter changed to a "large-figure" style in which highly animated peasants convey the rhythms and patterns of the dance. At about the same time Bruegel completed one of his most famous and beloved works, *Peasant Wedding Feast.* Expressing a spirit of sympathy and affection for country folk, this painting reveals the artist's delightful sense of humor as well as his genius in giving a universal meaning to even the most trivial events.

One of Bruegel's most disorienting works is *Land of Cockaigne* (1567). The composition is made up principally of three reclining figures—a knight, a peasant, and a burgher (mayor). These forms radiate outward from the center of the picture, producing a sensation of nausea and dislocation in the spectator. Art scholars suggest that the technique of tilting the ground and all of the other design elements reveal Bruegel's use of the mannerist style. *Parable of the Blind* (1568) illustrates verse 14 in chapter 14 of the Book of Matthew in the Bible: "If

Pieter Bruegel's most famous and beloved work, *Peasant Wedding Feast.* *Reproduced by permission of Art Resource.*

the blind lead the blind, both shall fall into the ditch." Another development of Bruegel's late period is a heightened sense of atmosphere in landscape paintings. This style is evident in what is probably his last work, *Magpie on the Gallows,* (1568) which he reportedly willed to his wife. At the center of the composition is a gallows (a device used for hanging people to death), which hovers over a group of dancing peasants. It forms a striking contrast to the beauties of the setting and serves as a grim reminder of the basic human condition.

Bruegel may have represented himself in a drawing titled *The Artist and the Connoisseur* (c. 1567), which portrays a cynical, embittered painter at work with an oafish, uncritical man watching him. The artist, who is probably Bruegel, makes no effort to disguise his contempt for the onlooker, whose conspicuous moneybag reveals his philistine nature (guided by materialism rather than true appreciation). Before his death Bruegel destroyed a number of his satirical drawings to save his wife from persecution. After his death his paintings and prints were endlessly copied and imitated. His peasant subjects and landscapes influenced later Netherlandish painters, including the great baroque (a term used to describe the music, art, literature, and philosophy of the seventeenth century; exuberant, sensuous, expressive, and dynamic style) artist **Peter Paul Rubens** (1577–1640; see entry). Bruegel's legacy was most directly transmitted through his two sons, Pieter the Younger (1564–1638) and Jan (1568–1625) who also became painters.

## For More Information

### Books

*Pieter Bruegel the Elder: Drawings and Prints*. New Haven, Conn.: Yale University Press, 2001.

### Web Sites

"Bruegel, Pieter the Elder." *Britannica.com*. [Online] Available http://www.britannica.com/eb/article?eu=17000&tocid=869&query=bruegel%2C%20pieter%20the%20elder, April 4, 2002.

Kren, Emil, and Daniel Marx. "Bruegel, Pieter the Elder." *Web Gallery of Art*. [Online] Available http://www.kfki.hu/~arthp/html/b/bruegel/pieter_e/index.html, April 4, 2002.

Pioch, Nicolas. "Bruegel, Pieter the Elder." *WebMuseum*. [Online] Available http://sunsite.unc.edu/wm/paint/auth/bruegel/, April 4, 2002.

# John Calvin

**July 10, 1509**
**Noyon, Picardy, France**
**May 27, 1564**
**Geneva, Switzerland**

**Theologian, religious leader**

"No one who wishes to be thought religious dares simply deny predestination, by which God adopts some to hope of life, and sentences others to eternal death."

*John Calvin quoted in* The Protestant Reformation, *edited by Hans J. Hillerbrand.*

**John Calvin.**
*Photograph courtesy of The Library of Congress.*

John Calvin was perhaps the most influential of all leaders of the Protestant Reformation, a movement to reform the Roman Catholic Church in Europe. He was involved in reform efforts at the same time as **Martin Luther** (1483–1546; see entry), the German priest who initiated the Reformation, but Calvin was twenty-six years younger than Luther. The two men developed some important theological differences. Significantly, Calvin's stern, "puritanical" interpretations of Christianity brought a renewed vigor to the Protestant Reformation, a religious reform movement within the Roman Catholic Church initiated by Luther in the early sixteenth century. Calvin established a distinct form of Protestantism—called "Calvinism"—at his base in Geneva, Switzerland. Calvinism proved to be adaptable to the current social and political changes in European society. Under his tireless direction, Geneva became the cosmopolitan focus of an effective and far-reaching evangelism (personal commitment to the teachings of Jesus Christ, founder of Christianity) to which many Protestant churches today owe their birth.

## Accepts Protestantism

John Calvin was born Jean Cauvin in Noyon, France, on July 10, 1509. His father, Gérard Cauvin, was an ambitious lawyer who worked for the local bishop. His mother, Jeanne Lefranc, was the daughter of a fairly well-to-do innkeeper. Calvin received his early education in Noyon until 1523, when he was awarded a benefice (church office in which income is used for education). He enrolled at the University of Paris, which was then the main center for the study of theology (religious doctrines and practices) in Europe. Calvin remained at Paris for five years with the intention of entering the priesthood, but in 1528 his father ordered him to switch his emphasis from theology to law. The reason for this was probably a matter of practicality, as more money could be made in the law than in the priesthood. Calvin obeyed his father's order and left Paris to study first at the University of Orléans, and later in Brouges, both located in France. Although he had already developed a passion for theology, Calvin embraced the study of law.

In 1532 Calvin published his first book, an edition of *De clementia* by the Roman political leader and philosopher Seneca (c. 4 B.C.–A.D. 65), which demonstrated his potential as an intellectual, and indicated a bright career. The death of his father earlier that year changed his life drastically and caused him to return to Paris. Calvin was now free to indulge his humanist and theological interests. (Humanism was the study of ancient Greek and Roman literature and language as well as early biblical texts, with the purpose of exploring the human capacity for achievement and improvement. Humanism was based on rhetoric, or effective speaking and writing, which provided momentum for the Renaissance.) He studied with several royal lecturers who introduced new humanistic ideas and disciplines into the intellectual community. Calvin, who already displayed a distinct moral uprightness, began to examine his own religious beliefs more fully. Despite being a Catholic, he accepted the Protestant doctrine emphasizing the omnipotence (supreme, unlimited power and presence) of God and felt a personal challenge to be an instrument of God's will.

## Embraces humanism

Calvin's first significant publication was *Commentary on Seneca's "De clementia,"* in which he expanded on the work of Dutch humanist and scholar **Desidius Erasmus** (1466–1536; see entry), who was influencing religious thought throughout Europe. Calvin's work displayed both his fluency in Latin and his ability to use Greek sources. He was clearly well educated in the classic traditions and the work of contemporary humanist commentators. In the intellectual community of the time, a dialogue had been ongoing between the humanists and scholastics. (Scholastics were scholars who followed a method developed in the Middle Ages, which sought to integrate Christian faith with the philosophy of reason found in the works of such ancient philosophers as Socrates, Plato, and Aristotle). Calvin's writing shows that he was a firm humanist rhetorician.

During this time, under circumstances which are still unknown, Calvin converted to Protestantism and began openly associating with other Protestants in and around Paris. Late in 1533 there was a general crackdown by the royal government on all Protestants, causing Calvin to flee Paris.

He left France altogether in 1534 and traveled under the assumed name Martianus Lucianius. He settled in Basel, Switzerland, and spent the next two years in private study, reading the works of Luther and Augustine (354–430), a founding father of the Catholic Church and an important early theologian. Calvin also met a number of men who shared his theological beliefs, giving him a sense of belonging to a community. In 1536 he published the first edition of his major work, *Christianae religionis institutio* (Institutes of the Christian Religion). The book explained the essentials of the Christian faith from a Protestant perspective for common readers, not theologians. He used basic language and avoided scholastic terms and traditions, hoping to gain favor for his new vision of the Christian faith. *Institutes,* which stated the essentials of Calvinist thought, gave Protestant theology a much-needed expression. It became the single most widely read and influential work of theology published in the Reformation period. *Institutes* marked Calvin as a religious leader of significance and authority. No Roman Catholic work of theology reached such a large audience, and Calvin spent much of the rest of his life revising, translating, and expanding the book. Final versions appeared in Latin in 1559 and in French in 1560.

*Institutes of the Christian Religion*

For John Calvin the only spiritual authority was scripture, found in both the New Testament and the Old Testament. According to his interpretation, God's omnipotence can be seen in what is called "predestination." Those who believed in predestination held that God had determined, from the beginning of time, who was to be saved and who was to be damned. Calvin believed that all people were sinful by nature, did not deserve redemption, and could not truly know God. It was through God's inexplicable mercy that the Elect (those chosen by God) were saved. Though this concept of predestination was to be stressed by some later "Calvinists," Calvin felt that the purpose of life was to strive to know or understand God as well as possible and then to follow God's will. This could be done only through faith in Jesus Christ which required all people to live a moral life. While there was no assurance of salvation, believers were given hope that they were among the Elect chosen by the omnipresent God. Calvin was severe in his efforts to abide by God's will, and he later founded a church that became an instrument of strict moral discipline.

## Establishes reform center

Due to the popularity of the *Institutes* and the strength of its theological ideas, Calvin was invited by the French reformer Guillaume Farel (1489–1565) to become a lecturer in Geneva in 1536. In June of that year Farel convinced Calvin that it was his duty to God to remain in Geneva. Farel claimed that it was God's will for Calvin to stay in Geneva to help expel the remaining elements of Catholicism from the area. The city had recently won its independence from the Catholic Church and Farel saw an opportunity to gain support for Calvin's brand of Christianity. Despite his dislike for the city and its politics, Calvin would focus most of his ministry on Geneva for the rest of his life. Together Farel and Calvin directed the Reformation in the city, hoping to fully establish Protestantism as part of a total moral reform and to eliminate the lack of discipline associated with Catholicism. However, within a couple of years both men were expelled because of their moral strictness and their encouragement of French immigration into the city. Calvin was not bothered by the expulsion, feeling that it simply meant freedom from the burden of politics and ministry. He went

on to Strassburg, France, where he taught at an academy, preached, and developed his ideas on the nature of the ideal Christian church.

In August 1540, upon the urging of friends in Strassburg, Calvin married Idelette Bure, the widow of one of his converts. Bure already had a son and a daughter from her previous marriage, the only child she had with Calvin died shortly after birth in 1542. Bure died seven years later, and Calvin never remarried. Little is known of their life together, though Calvin's relations with women were not entirely warm. Due to his outspoken criticism, most of his vocal opponents were women.

## Calvin returns to Geneva

In 1541 Calvin reluctantly returned to Geneva in response to a call from the now floundering Protestant church. He was assured that he would be given the freedom

## Calvin Executes Servetus

In 1553, Michael Servetus (1511–1553), a Spanish scientist, humanist, and theologian, arrived in Geneva. He was traveling in disguise to avoid persecution for his scandalous religious ideas. Often called the first Unitarian (a present-day Protestant denomination), Servetus denied the divinity (godliness) of Christ and the doctrine of the Trinity (the Christian concept of God as the Father, the Son, and the Holy Spirit). He believed that God was a single, indivisible divine force. His views alienated him from both Catholics and Protestants. When Calvin recognized Servetus sitting within the crowd listening to one of his sermons, he promptly had Servetus arrested and put on trial. As the "Defender of the Faith," Calvin demanded that Servetus be executed. His order was supported by the Geneva city government, and on October 27, 1553, Servetus was burned alive for heresy (violation of the laws of God).

he felt was necessary to build God's earthly kingdom. He soon organized the local church government outlined in his work titled *Ecclesiastical Ordinances* (1545). He began to develop a well-regulated social network within a morally disciplined society. Despite considerable opposition within the city, Calvin's influence grew steadily. He defeated theological and political opponents alike (see accompanying box). Calvin overcame most remaining opposition to his plans and in 1555 his group called the Consistory, which acted as a sort of moral court, was accepted and given great powers by the city. From that point on moral discipline was strictly enforced in Geneva. Taverns were closed and replaced with *abbayes* in which patrons were closely watched for signs of excessive drinking and rowdy behavior. Throughout Geneva, citizens monitored one another's conduct, ready to report any sort of wrongdoing. A strict moral order, based on Calvin's particular vision of Christianity, eventually emerged in the city. Calvin associated himself with godliness and truth in every battle, religious or otherwise. Thus, for him, to tolerate opposition of any kind was to tolerate evil. Though Calvin was particularly enthusiastic in enforcing his will, it must be remembered that he was not entirely unlike his sixteenth-century contemporaries in their intolerance of dissent.

Constantly preaching and writing, Calvin involved himself in all aspects of civic affairs in Geneva, including education, trade, diplomacy, and even sanitation. In 1559 he established the Genevan Academy (now the University of Geneva) for the training of clergy. Calvin was also interested in the spread of the Reformation movement abroad, especially within his native France. Under his direction Geneva became a haven for persecuted Protestants and the unofficial center of growing Protestant movements in places as far removed as Scotland. Calvin's constant activity was a major factor in his failing health. In 1558 he had suffered an attack of pleurisy (disease of the lungs), and later, after delivering a sermon, began to cough blood. By 1563 he was effectively bedridden. Yet Calvin remained true to his moral standards and dutifully bound to his ethic of hard work, determined to continue his mission in whatever manner possible. On May 27, 1564, he died of pulmonary tuberculosis (severe lung disease).

## For More Information

### Books

Greef, Wulfert de. *The Writings of John Calvin: An Introductory Guide,* Lyle D. Bierma, translator. Grand Rapids, Mich.: Baker Books, 1993.

Hillerbrand, Hans J., ed. *The Protestant Reformation.* New York: Peter Smith Publisher, 1992.

Parker, T. H. L. *John Calvin, a Biography.* Philadelphia: Westminster Press, 1975.

### Web Sites

"Calvin, John." *Encyclopedia.com.* [Online] Available http://www.ency clopedia.com/searchpool.asp?target=@DOCTITLE%20Calvin%20%2 0John, April 4, 2002.

# Baldassare Castiglione

**December 6, 1478**
**Casatico, Mantua, Italy**
**February 7, 1529**
**Toledo, Spain**

**Diplomat, author, courtier**

The Italian author, courtier, and diplomat Baldassare Castiglione was one of the most influential writers of the Renaissance. The Renaissance was a cultural movement initiated by scholars called humanists, who promoted the revival of the human-centered literature and philosophy of ancient Greece and Rome as well as new translations of biblical texts (Hebrew holy books and the Christian Bible). He ranks with the English playwright and poet **William Shakespeare** (1564–1616; see entry) and the French essayist **Michel de Montaigne** (1533–1592; see entry) in importance to the literature of Europe. Castiglione is known primarily for *Book of the Courtier,* in which he portrayed the ideal courtier (gentlemen of the court). This work was a chief vehicle in spreading Italian humanism into England and France. (Humanism was a movement that originated in Florence, Italy. It was based on a renewed appreciation of the values of ancient Greek and Roman civilization, emphasizing the human potential for achievement and improvement. Humanism was the motivating force for the Renaissance.)

"It is better to pass in silence that which cannot be recalled without pain."

*Baldassare Castiglione in* Book of the Courtier.

**Baldassare Castiglione.**
*Photograph courtesy of The Library of Congress.*

## Serves as courtier

Baldassare Castiglione was born on December 6, 1478, in Casatico, Italy, located in the province of Mantua. He belonged to an illustrious family in Lombardy, a region in northern Italy. After receiving a classical education in Mantua and in Milan, he served at the court of Lodovico Sforza (1452–1508), duke of Milan, from 1496 to 1499. When his father died in 1499, Castiglione returned to Mantua and entered the service of Francesco Gonzaga (1466–1519), duke of Mantua. In 1503 he fought with Gonzaga's forces against the Spanish in Naples. On his way north he stopped in Rome and Urbino. Both cities fascinated him. His request to transfer to the court of Guidobaldo da Montefeltro (1472–1508), duke of Urbino, was grudgingly granted in 1504 by Gonzaga.

At Urbino, Castiglione participated in intellectual discussions headed by Guidobaldo's wife, Elizabetta, duchess of Urbino. He wrote a dramatic work, *Tirsi,* for a carnival at Urbino in 1506. The work is a celebration of the court of Guidobaldo, the duchess, and many friends who would figure prominently in *Book of the Courtier.* Castiglione's service in Urbino gave him access to the court of Pope Julius II (1443–1513; reigned 1503–1513), where he became a friend of the Italian artist **Raphael** (1483–1520; see entry).

After Guidobaldo's death in 1508, Castiglione remained in the service of the duke's successor, Francesco Maria della Rovere (1490–1538), and participated in Urbino's military actions. He also organized the first performance of *Calandria* (Follies of Calandro), a comedy (humorous play) by the Italian cardinal and playwright Bernardo Dovisi (called Bibiena; 1470–1520). Castiglione wrote a prologue (introduction) to the work, which is now lost. In 1513 he was named count of Nuvolara by Rovere. Three years later he married, but became a cleric (church official) in 1521 after the death of his wife. In 1524 he was sent by Pope Clement VII (1478–1534; reigned 1523–34) as ambassador to the court of Holy Roman Emperor **Charles V** (1500–1558; see entry) in Spain. The mission proved to be unfortunate, as Castiglione wrongly reported the emperor's intentions in the period leading up to the sack (destruction) of Rome by Charles's army in 1527.

## Book of the Courtier is great success

*Book of the Courtier* was published in 1528, though Castiglione developed the main idea at the court of Urbino in 1507 and wrote it from 1513 to 1516. The work was a huge and immediate success. It consists of four sections, or books, in which Castiglione blended classical learning into the format of polite conversation among courtiers and their ladies. He featured real-life figures as participants in the conversations.

In Book One the assembled courtiers and ladies propose games for their entertainment and decide to "portray in words a perfect courtier." All participants "will be permitted to contradict the speaker as in the schools of the [ancient] philosophers." Discussions are led by Ludovico da Canossa (1476–1532), a diplomat from Verona, Italy, and a relative of Castiglione. The participants decide that the courtier should be noble, witty, and pleasant. He should be an accomplished horseman and a warrior (his principal profession) who is devoted to his prince. He should know Greek, Latin, French, and Spanish, and he should be skilled in literature, music, painting, and dancing. The courtier's behavior should be characterized by grace and ease, and he should carefully avoid any affectation.

A courtier bidding his lady farewell before going to battle. Baldassare Castiglione's *Book of the Courtier* described this as being proper behavior for courtiers and their ladies. *©Christie's Images/Corbis. Reproduced by permission of Corbis Corporation.*

Book Two is a treatment of the ways and circumstances in which the ideal courtier might demonstrate his qualities. It stresses decorum (proper behavior) and conversational skills. At first Federico Fregoso (died 1541), cardinal and archbishop of Salerno, presides over the discussion. When the topic turns to humorous language, Bibiena takes over. The participants then engage in humorous stories, pleasantries, and practical jokes. Book Three defines the qualities of a suitable female companion for the perfect courtier. Leading the discussions and defending women against attack is Giuliano de' Medici (1479–1516), son of **Lorenzo de' Medici** (1449–1492; see entry) and brother of Pope Leo X (1475–1521; reigned 1513–21). The participants discuss the virtue of women, giving ancient and contemporary examples and telling entertaining stories. They give the lady of the palace many of the same qualities as the courtier. Physical beauty is more important to her, however, and she must always be more discreet in order to preserve her good reputation. In this book the voices of the assembled ladies are heard more often, but here, as in the other three books, women only ask questions. Although they lead the discussions, they are never active participants.

Book Four begins with a long discussion of the courtier's primary role as an adviser to his prince. The participants conclude that the courtier must earn the favor of the prince through his accomplishments. He must win his master's trust so completely that he can always speak truthfully without fear. He can even correct the prince if necessary. This subject leads to a debate of the merits of republics (governments ruled by representatives of the people) and monarchies. The topic of conversation finally turns to love, picking up a theme introduced in Book Three. Here the discussion centers on how the courtier, who is no longer young, should love. Pietro Bembo (1470–1547), a noted authority on the subject, instructs the assembled party on a humanist theory of love based on the works of Plato. Bembo explains, step by step, the way to rise from a vision of human beauty to an understanding of ideal beauty, and from there to God. As he speaks he seems to lose touch with his surroundings, and one of the participants tugs at his shirt to awaken him from his reverie.

## Helps spread humanism

Castiglione's idealized picture of society at the court of Urbino quickly became a book of etiquette (rules for proper manners) for both the bourgeoisie (middle class) and the aristocracy (upper class) all over Europe. It was translated into Spanish in 1534; French in 1537; English in 1561; and German in 1566. *Book of the Courtier* was printed in forty editions in the sixteenth century alone and one hundred more by 1900. Through it the broad values of Italian humanism, focusing on the ideal of the fully developed, well-rounded

## A "portrait of the court of Urbino"

*Book of the Courtier* is based on Baldassare Castiglione's experiences at the court of Urbino. It depicts conversations that took place in 1506, and many of the participants are courtiers and ladies whom Castiglione met during the years he spent in Urbino. In the letter that opens the book, Castiglione looked back on those days with nostalgia, remembering with admiration and love the friends who had died. He called his book a "portrait of the court of Urbino," through which he intended to preserve their memory. He imagined that the conversations were held during his absence in 1506, when Pope Julius and his attendants stopped at Urbino. This technique allowed Castiglione to include in the book participants who were not members of the court at the time. It also enabled him to remove himself from the discussions, which he claimed to narrate as they were reported to him.

In the opening letter Castiglione defended his use of a language that is not Tuscan, the only Italian dialect (a variety of a language spoken in a particular region or by a particular group) considered appropriate to literature during the Renaissance. Instead, he wrote in the language used by educated persons throughout the Italian peninsula. This emphasis on language may explain why the letter was addressed to Don Michel de Silva, a Portuguese diplomat and friend of Castiglione. Silva was interested in discussions of the Italian language. Castiglione dedicated *Book of the Courtier* to Alfonso Ariosto, a close friend. Ariosto had urged him on behalf of King Francis I (1494–1547; ruled 1515–47) of France to write a work on the subject of the perfect courtier.

courtier and his lady, were spread throughout western Europe. Yet it must be admitted that in *Book of the Courtier* the high ideals of *humanitas,* or culture and virtue, are elevated not for themselves but as tools of self-advancement.

Castiglione died in Toledo, Spain, on February. 7, 1529. His name lived on in *Book of the Courtier,* which is still being read in the twenty-first century. Castiglione was characterized by many as a dignified, melancholy, and idealistic man, qualities that Raphael captured in his famous portrait of the author. As a writer, Castiglione tended to soften the rough edges of society and to avoid moral issues. For instance, he said of the Italians' recent dismal military performance, it is better to avoid disturbing issues than to continually bring them up. Another example of his treatment of social matters can be seen in his answer to the question of what a courtier should do when ordered by his prince to commit an immoral act such as murder. In *Book of the Courtier* Castiglione stated: "There would be too much to say; it must all be left to your discretion." Despite avoiding complex moral and social issues, there is much that is positive in the book. Castiglione elevated the concept of human personality and dignity, and he praised the creative possibilities of humankind. Only a modest poet in both Italian and Latin, he wrote a fine sonnet (a fourteen-line poem having one of several conventional rhyme schemes) on the ruins of Rome, *Superbicolli e voi sacre ruine*. It reappears in the *Antiquités de Rome*, by French poet Joachim du Bellay (1522–1560), and in *Ruines of Rome*, by the English poet Edmund Spenser (c. 1552–1599). Castiglione's poetry was published in 1760 and his letters in 1769 and 1771.

## For More Information

### Books

Castiglione, Baldassare. *Book of the Courtier; An Authoritative Text, Criticism*. Daniel Javitch, ed. New York: Norton, 2002.

### Web Sites

"Baldassare Castiglione [portrait] by Raphael." *Great Artists in History*. [Online] Available http://www.theartgallery.com.au/ArtEducation/ greatartists/Raphael/baldassare/, April 4, 2002.

"Castiglione, Baldassare." *Encyclopedia.com*. [Online] Available http:// www.encyclopedia.com/articlesnew/02398.html, April 4, 2002.

# Catherine de Médicis

**1519
Florence, Italy
1589
Paris, France**

**Regent, queen**

Catherine de Médicis was never able to rule France as its monarch because of the Salic Law, which restricted royal succession solely to men. Despite this law, she reigned as regent (one who rules in place of a young monarch) for nearly thirty years and did everything she could to strengthen the positions of her three weak sons. She presided over, and was partly responsible for, many of the horrors of the French Wars of Religion in the 1560s and 1570s. The worst of these was the massacre of Protestants gathered in Paris to witness the marriage of her daughter Margaret Valois to Duke Henry of Navarre in 1572. Catherine's calculating policies yielded short-term victories, but when she died in 1589 her hopes for her family's long-term future lay in ruins.

## Marries at fourteen

Catherine was born in 1519, daughter of **Lorenzo de' Medici** (1449–1492; see entry), the powerful duke of Florence, Italy. Her mother died within a few days from puerperal fever (an infection that can follow childbirth) and her fa-

Catherine de Médicis.
*©Bettmann/Corbis.
Reproduced by permission of
Corbis Corporation.*

ther succumbed to consumption (pulmonary tuberculosis) a week later. Catherine was thus an orphan after less than one month of life. Her father's relatives, among them popes Leo X (1475–1521; reigned 1513–21) and Clement VII (1478–1534; reigned 1523–34), took over her care, and she grew up in the midst of the stormy Italian Wars (1494–1559), a conflict between France and Spain over control of Italy. When a German army of the Holy Roman Emperor **Charles V** (1500–1558; see entry) sacked (destroyed) Rome in 1527, the citizens of Florence took advantage of this eclipse of Medici power to restore their republic. They held Pope Clement prisoner in the papal castle in Rome. Eight-year-old Catherine was taken hostage in Florence. Clement managed to escape from Rome and hired a group of mercenaries (professional soldiers) to recapture Florence. They rescued Catherine, who had been hiding in a convent (house for women who are dedicated to religious life).

To assist her uncle Clement VII's political ambitions, fourteen-year-old Catherine was married in 1533 to fourteen-year-old Henry (later Henry II 1519–1559; ruled 1547–59), duke of Orléans, younger son of **Francis I** king of France (1494–1547; see entry). The elaborate wedding ceremony at Marseilles Cathedral was conducted by the pope himself. The death of her husband's older brother in 1536 made Henry and Catherine heirs to the throne, but the circumstances of his death made Catherine unpopular. One of the members of her court, Count Sebastian Montecuculi, was suspected of poisoning him to promote the interests of Catherine and, possibly, of France's enemy Charles V.

Catherine was unable to conceive a child for the first ten years of marriage, which made her even more unpopular in the French court. In her efforts to become pregnant Catherine consulted astrologers (those who predict future events according to the positions of celestial bodies)—among them the famous French physician and astronomer **Nostradamus** (1503–1566; see entry). When she finally gave birth to the first of ten children in 1543, she believed the astrologers had helped her overcome her infertility. Seven of Catherine's children survived, and she outlived all but one, the future King Henry III (1551–1589; ruled 1574–89), who would follow her to the grave in a matter of months. Throughout her life Catherine maintained a fierce belief in astrology, necromancy

**Catherine, Henry, and Diane**

When Catherine's husband, King Henry II, was a child he was held hostage with his father, King Francis I, at the Spanish court in Madrid. At that time France and Spain were in the midst of the Italian Wars over the control of Italy. On Henry's return, at age eleven, he had been cared for by Diane de Poitiers (1499–1566), who was twenty years his senior. Despite the age difference they became lovers, and throughout most of Henry's reign, which began in 1547, Diane completely eclipsed Catherine in influence over the king. Nevertheless, Catherine and Diane maintained friendly relations. The age difference and Diane's lack of beauty made Henry's attraction and loyalty to her something of a mystery at court. Diane was even given responsibility for raising the royal couple's children, and she and Henry arranged the betrothal of Henry and Catherine's oldest son, Francis, to Mary Stuart (Mary, Queen of Scots) in 1548. By 1557, however, Catherine's coolness in an emergency won her new respect from Henry. After he had lost the battle of Saint Quentin to Philip II king of Spain, Paris was placed in jeopardy. Catherine made a patriotic speech to the Parliament (ruling body of France), persuading it to raise more troops and money to continue the fight. Thus she put to rest the old suspicion that she was more an Italian schemer than a true queen of France.

(contacting spirits of the dead to reveal the future or influence events), and astronomy (scientific study of heavenly bodies). She was also an active patron of Nostradamus.

## Wars of Religion begin

At the time of Catherine's birth in 1519, the Protestant Reformation had been underway for two years. In 1517 the German monk **Martin Luther** (1483–1546; see entry) delivered charges of corruption against the Roman Catholic Church. The challenge to Rome's religious dominance quickly gained momentum in Germany and soon spread throughout Europe. The French theologian and Protestant reformer **John Calvin** (1509–1564; see entry), living and writing in Geneva, Switzerland, was particularly inspiring to many French men and women. They saw in his teachings a version of Christianity truer to their faith, one they believed was not as politicized and corrupt as the Catholic Church. French Protestants were known as Huguenots, and the rapid growth of their numbers among the nobility and upper classes as well as among ordinary people soon made them a politically significant force. The Huguenots held their first general French assembly in 1559.

During this era European monarchs were determined to rule their kingdoms under the authority of one church or faith. The religious division between the Huguenots and the Catholics in France was unusual. The Catholic monarchs of France and Spain made peace at Cateau-Cambrésis in 1559, partly because they were bankrupt but also so that they could unite their forces against Protestantism. The treaty was symbolically sealed by the marriage of Philip II of Spain (1527–1598) to Elisabeth of Valois (1545–1568), the teenaged daughter of Catherine and Henry. At the joust held to mark the wedding celebrations on June 28, 1559, Henry was injured by a lance wielded by a Calvinist nobleman, the Comte Gabriel de Montgomery (c. 1530–1574). The lance shattered the king's helmet, pierced his eye, and entered his brain. The blinded king died ten days later. Nostradamus had supposedly foreseen this event and had written about it in Quatrain 35 of his popular book *Centuries I.* The prophesy stated: "The young lion will overcome the older one/ On the field of combat in single battle/ He will pierce his eyes through a golden cage/ Two wounds made one, then he dies a cruel death." Summoned to the royal court in 1556, Nostradamus told the king to avoid any ceremonial jousting during his forty-first year (1559). This warning had been given by Henry's own astrologer as well. While at court, Nostradamus had also drawn up astrology charts for four of the royal couple's sons and predicted that they all would become kings.

Henry's death brought his and Catherine's oldest son, sixteen-year-old Francis II (1544–1560; ruled 1559–60), to the throne. Francis had married Mary Stuart (Queen of Scots; 1542–1587) the previous year. He inherited a country full of demobilized soldiers, many of them unpaid for months. Tax burdens on the peasants were heavy, allowing Calvinist preachers spreading the message of an uncorrupted faith to find a receptive audience. Huguenot noblemen took action almost at once, organizing a conspiracy to overthrow or at least dominate the court of Francis. They won the active support of England's new Protestant queen, **Elizabeth I** (1533–1603; see entry). Then, at the city of Amboise, France, their military uprising failed and the royal army then arrested the leaders. In the presence of Catherine, her children, and Queen Mary, fifty-seven of the Huguenot leaders were hanged or beheaded. This retribution did not end the religious and political conflicts plaguing France, however. From that time forward the Huguenot Navarre family and the Catholic Guises led rival religious and court factions. The death of Francis II in December 1560 made Catherine regent for her second son Charles, who now became King Charles IX (1550–1574; ruled 1560–74) at the age of ten.

## Leads political maneuvers

Charles IX was an unstable man, even as a young child. While he was growing up he came to dislike his mother and her favorite, younger son Henry. Catherine found it easy to dominate Charles despite his growing resentment. As the French monarchy continued to deal with the constant warfare, Catherine tried to carve some order out of the financial and administrative chaos of the kingdom. Her ultimate goal was to strengthen the country for her sons' reigns. In 1565 she joined in a meeting led by her son-in-law, Philip II of Spain, to discuss the continuing religious crisis. Philip disliked her apparent willingness to pit Catholics and Protestants against one another. In Philip's view she should have been doing more to advance the Catholic Reformation (also called the Counter Reformation), a reform movement within the church. He also knew that France's weakness was a strategic benefit for Spain. It made the possibility of French aid to Dutch rebels against Spain far less likely. When Philip's wife and Catherine's favorite daughter Elisabeth died in childbirth in 1568, Catherine hoped he might marry her younger daughter Margaret. Philip had no plans to wed Margaret, for he was determined to sever his connection with France. A further blow to Catherine's political maneuvering came the same year when her daughter-in-law, Mary, Queen of Scots, was captured by her English enemies and imprisoned. This left Scotland open to Protestant domination and effectively ended a French-Scottish Catholic encirclement of England.

Although Catherine was a lifelong Catholic, she always had a degree of religious cynicism (doubt tinged with contempt). She never understood the passion that many of her contemporaries brought to their faith. For Catherine, religious differences were mainly bargaining chips that could be used in court politics. Her appointment of Admiral Gaspard de Coligny (1519–1572), an influential Huguenot, to act as Charles's chief advisor, is a perfect example of her desire to play both sides of the field. This appointment provoked members of the powerful Guise family—François of Lorraine, duke of Guise (1519–1563), and Charles of Guise, cardinal of Lorraine (c. 1525–1574)—to join the constable of France in a Catholic alliance against Coligny and the Protestants. In 1561 Catherine called the Colloquy, of Poissy, a conference of Roman Catholic prelates (cardinals and bishops) and Protestant ministers (heads of congregations). Once again she tried to broker peace between the Catholic faction, led by the cardinal of Lorraine, and the Huguenots, under the reform theologian and Calvin's friend, Theodore Beza (1519–1605). Far from coming to an understanding with one another, the two parties hardened their differences. Soon hostilities erupted in the poisoned atmosphere of broken negotiation.

Catherine issued the Edict (royal order) of January in 1562, which allowed a limited relationship between Huguenots and Catholics in France. Protestants welcomed the edict, but the Catholic rejection of it ultimately led the country into four decades of civil war, often called the French Wars of Religion. With the official outbreak of war, Catherine allied herself with François duke of Guise. The situation, both in the court and on the battlefield, was further complicated when Coligny ordered the assassination of the duke of Guise in 1563. Wanting to end the war, Catherine oversaw the negotiations that resulted in Edict of Amboise in March 1563. This new edict was essentially a reworking of the Edict of January, meant to satisfy all powers involved. Despite these efforts the Huguenots and the Catholics renewed their hostilities, resulting in second and third civil wars. Although Catherine was able to end the second war (September 1567–March 1568) with the Peace of Longjumeau (a reworking of the Edict of Amboise), the peace was short-lived. Fighting resumed in August 1568. As the fighting continued from 1568 to 1570, Huguenot armies attacked convents and monasteries, torturing and massacring their inhabitants. Catholic forces, equally merciless, murdered the Huguenots of several districts indiscriminately. After the conclusion of the third civil war in August 1570, the Peace of Saint Germain was signed.

## Uneasy peace shattered

The treaty temporarily reconciled the two sides and led to Coligny's return to court. Among the treaty's provisions was the specification that Catherine's daughter Margaret of Valois (1553–1615) should marry Henry of Navarre, the Huguenot leader and later Henry IV (1553–1610; ruled 1572–1610), first Bourbon king of France (see accompanying box). The Huguenots were also to be given several strongholds throughout France, and Coligny was permitted to resume his position as a royal councilor. Catherine hoped that, as a moderate Huguenot, he might act to pacify his fellow Protestants while she played the same role among Catholics. Catherine's plan did not work, however. Coligny quickly and brutishly reasserted himself at court, becoming a friend and confidante of King Charles IX. Despite being friends with the king, Coligny aroused suspicions among Catholic courtiers and many thought he was planning another coup (violent overthrow of the government). When Coligny discovered that Charles and his mother were at odds, he sided with the king, an action that provoked Catherine's furious resentment.

Catherine decided to dispose of Coligny once and for all. She accepted an offer from the Guise party to assassinate him, hoping that the outcome would be revived power for her own party. The assassin shot Coligny but failed to kill him, and Charles IX rushed to his side, promising a full inquiry and retribution against the assassins. Catherine and Charles's younger brother Henry quickly interceded and convinced Charles that Coligny was manipulating him. They told him that Coligny planned to overthrow the whole Catholic court, and the only solution was to assassinate him and the other Huguenot leaders.

By careful prearrangement church bells began to ring at two in the morning of August 24, 1572, Saint Bartholomew's Day. The bells signaled Catholic troops to move in and kill the injured Coligny and other Huguenot leaders. While the original plan called for precise and specific assassinations, the attacks quickly became indiscriminate and all sense of order

## Like Mother, Like Daughter

After a decade of religious war, the city of Paris had remained friendly to the ultra-Catholic Guise party and most Parisians resented the concessions given to Huguenots at the Peace of Saint Germain. When a large Huguenot assembly entered the city in the summer of 1572 to celebrate the wedding of Margaret of Valois to Henry of Navarre, the population was restless and angry. Margaret took after her mother and was well known for her stormy personality and court intrigues. The relationship between mother and daughter was not always strong, however. Years earlier, when Catherine had discovered that Margaret was having an affair with Charles of Guise, she and King Charles IX beat the girl senseless. Catherine did almost everything for self-serving reasons, which included using members of her own family for political gain. The motive for this marriage alliance was that Henry of Navarre, a Huguenot, would have a strong claim to the French throne if neither Charles IX nor Catherine's younger son Henry had a living heir. A connection to the Valois family would strengthen Navarre's claim to the throne, and it would increase Catherine's prospects of continued influence. Margaret, however, was still in love with Guise and resisted the planned marriage. She and Henry of Navarre had known each other for many years and they realized there was no sexual attraction between them. Margaret was notoriously clean and Henry often refused to bathe for months at a time. To further complicate matters, Margaret refused to give up her Catholic faith for this marriage. When Henry's mother, Jeanne of Navarre, died suddenly during the negotiations for the wedding, many Huguenots were ready to believe that Catherine poisoned Jeanne. This suspicion was apparently unfounded, however.

broke down. As widespread looting and fighting broke out across Paris, more than two thousand men, women, and children (including many people uninvolved in political and religious controversy) were shot or hacked to death. Similar massacres followed in the provinces as Catholics seized the initiative against their local Huguenot rivals. King Charles feared that he had unleashed a revolution. Catherine, however, was extremely pleased. A fourth civil war at once began, but a strange turn of events altered the course of the war. Leadership of the Huguenot party now fell to Catherine's youngest and most unscrupulous son, Francis, duke of Alençon and Anjou (1554–1584). Francis placed himself at the head of the Protestant forces. He had hopes of succeeding Charles as king because their brother Henry had just been elected king of Poland and was no longer in line for the French throne.

## Henry asserts himself

Henry, Catherine's third son, was less easily dominated and manipulated than Charles. Henry had spent the 1560s garnering the laurels of a successful general in the wars against the Huguenots. His victories won him the envy of King Charles IX, whose physical frailty forbade fighting in wars. Catherine tried to marry Henry to Elizabeth I of England, but the "Virgin Queen" (as Elizabeth became known) tactfully declined the offer. She also refused a marriage proposal from Francis, the new leader of the Protestant forces, whom she referred to as the "frog."

Henry did not want to go to Poland, even though his mother had gone through great pains to secure him the throne. Finally, despite his objections, Henry set out for Poland. His departure prompted another Huguenot uprising, in which Alençon, Henry of Navarre, and Margaret of Valois were all implicated as conspirators. With her usual energy, Catherine coordinated forces to quell it, and with her decisiveness, she witnessed the executions of the ringleaders. Shortly thereafter King Charles died at age twenty-four. Catherine now recalled Henry to claim his hereditary kingdom without opposition.

Henry III was crowned in 1575 and married in the same year to Louise of Lorraine. They had no children to carry on the Valois line. From this time on, Catherine entrusted family fortunes more wholeheartedly to the Catholic Guise family. In 1576 she approved the formation of the Catholic League, which marched to triumph against the Huguenots. Henry's homosexual favorites predominated at court. When the Guises provoked a duel and killed two of them, Henry was filled with hatred against the Guises. Another round of feuding began despite Catherine's continued urging that Henry must settle his differences with the Guises for the sake of national and Catholic security.

## Catherine's dreams are dashed

Catherine remained politically active until the end of her life, touring France on Henry's behalf and trying to assure

**The Tuileries Palace was originally built for Catherine, but the palace was not completed until the early seventeenth century. Although the building was destroyed in 1871, the famous gardens still remain.**
*Reproduced by permission of Hulton Archive.*

the loyalty of its many fractured and war-torn provinces. She also amassed a huge collection of books and paintings, built or enlarged some of Paris's finest buildings, including the Tuileries Palace. An active patron of the arts, Catherine helped to bring a new Italian dance form, the ballet, to France. Called *ballet de cour,* it was a forerunner to modern ballet and mixed theater performances, voices, and instruments. The first example of the French *ballet de cour* was *Ballet de Royne,* which was performed in 1581. To the end, Catherine carried on her fascination with astrology. By 1589 she was overweight and suffering from gout (inflammation of the joints and excessive uric acid in the blood), and had taken ill from the exertions of dancing at the wedding of one of her granddaughters. Catherine lived just long enough to hear that Henry's bodyguards had murdered Charles of Guise. The news broke her spirits, causing her to regard herself as an absolute failure. Everything she had worked for was destroyed by the only son she trusted to continue the family line. Later that year, Henry III in turn died, assassinated by Dominican friar (member of the Catholic order founded by Saint Dominic), Jacques Clement (1564–1589). Clement had regarded Henry as a traitor to the faith for joining Henry of Navarre against the Catholic League. In this way, the Valois dynasty came to an end. Ironically it was the Huguenot prince Henry of Navarre who succeeded to the throne, though he was unable to take power until 1593, when he half-heartedly converted to Catholicism.

Researchers throughout the ages have benefited from Catherine's scholarly interests. Her personal library contained numerous rare manuscripts, which were eventually placed in a museum. Through her interest in politics and the arts, Catherine left a lasting mark on French history and culture. Though regarded by many as a cruel and calculating woman, Catherine made an undeniable contribution to her adopted country.

## For More Information

### Books

Riley, Judith Merkle. *The Master of All Desires*. New York: Viking, 1999.

Roessner, Michaela. *The Stars Dispose*. New York: Tor, 1997.

Strage, Mark. *Women of Power: The Life and Times of Catherine de Médici*. New York: Harcourt Brace Jovanovich, 1976.

### Web Sites

"Catherine De Médicis." *Britannica.com*. [Online] Available http://www.britannica.com/search?query=catherine%20de%27%20medicis&ct=, April 4, 2002.

"Nostradamus." *MSN Encarta*. [Online] Available http://encarta.msn.com/find/Concise.asp?z=1&pg=2&ti=761568156, April 4, 2002.

# Margaret Cavendish

**1624**
**Colchester, England**
**1674**
**Nottinghamshire, England**

**Writer and intellectual**

"And although I have neither the power, time nor occasion to conquer the world as Alexander and Caesar did; yet rather than not to be mistress of one, since Fortune and the Fates would give me none, I have made a world of my own."

*Margaret Cavendish as quoted in* Blazing World *edited by Kate Lilley.*

**Margaret Cavendish.**
*©Bettmann/Corbis.*
*Reproduced by permission of*
*Corbis Corporation.*

The English author and intellectual Margaret Cavendish, first duchess of Newcastle, wrote in the greatest variety of genres of any women, or even men, of the late Renaissance period. Initiated by humanist scholars, the Renaissance was a movement that promoted the revival of the human-centered literature and philosophy of ancient Greece and Rome as well as new translations of biblical texts (Hebrew holy books and the Christian Bible). She sought fame through her works, but during her own lifetime she was a social outsider. Nicknamed "Mad Madge," she was ridiculed for her self-promotion, her willingness to debate famous male thinkers, and her strong feminist views.

## Meets husband in exile

Cavendish was born Margaret Lucas in 1624 in Colchester, England, to Thomas Lucas, a wealthy landowner, and his wife. Margaret was the youngest of eight children in an extraordinarily close family. Even as adults she and her brothers and sisters often spent time together in London. Margaret's life was significantly influenced by her siblings' encouragement and her mother's management of the family property after Thomas Lucas's death in 1625. Cavendish wrote in her autobiography: "And though she [her mother] would often complain that her family was too great for her weak management ... yet I observe she took pleasure and some little pride, in the governing thereof." Cavendish's long writing career, and her questioning of the roles and expectations for women, were the most distinguishing characteristics of her own life.

In 1642 the English Civil War (1642–48) broke out when rebel forces overthrew King Charles I (1600–1669; ruled 1625–49). The Lucases moved to the royalist (pro-monarchy) town of Oxford, south of London, where Margaret was appointed maid of honor at the court of Queen Henrietta Maria (1609–1669). Two years later Margaret accompanied the queen into exile (forced absence from one's country) in Paris, France. By 1645 she had met William Cavendish (1592–1676), duke of Newcastle. Although Newcastle had recently led the deposed (no longer in power) king's forces in an unsuccessful campaign at Marston Moor, he came to court as a royalist hero. Thirty years older than Margaret, he was also an eligible widower, his wife having just died during childbirth. Over the objections of the queen and Newcastle's friends, the couple wed within six months and remained in Paris.

Over the objections of her mother and her friends, Margaret married William Cavendish, duke of Newcastle. *Reproduced by permission of Hulton Archive.*

## Starts writing career

King Charles I was beheaded in 1649 and the Commonwealth government was established in England. Newcastle was officially banished from the country and his property was seized. He and Margaret went to Antwerp, Belgium, where they lived in exile. In 1651 Margaret went back to England with her brother-in-law Charles Cavendish to seek repayment for William's estate. The request was denied. While she was in England for nearly two years Margaret wrote her first works, *Poems, and Fancies* and *Philosophical Fancies*, which were both issued in 1653. Not only did she take the daring step of becoming a published author—English women rarely wrote for a public audience at the time—but she also signed her own name to her books. (It was customary at the time for female authors to use male "pen names," or aliases, to protect the identity of their gender.) After returning to Antwerp in 1653, she wrote four more books, thus beginning a productive, twenty-year writing career. The Newcastles went back to England in 1660, when Charles II (1630–1685; ruled 1660–85) took the throne at the beginning of the Restoration (reinstatement of the monarchy). They settled at William's estate, Welbeck in Nottinghamshire.

## Ridiculed by contemporaries

Cavendish's works received a mixed reception—more negative than positive—during her lifetime, and have continued to gain mixed reviews ever since. More recently scholars have approached her as a writer of fantasy, autobiography, and biography. She is also regarded as a marginally successful writer of scientific works. Nevertheless, Cavendish produced a more substantial body of work than any other mid-seventeenth-century woman. She wrote in the greatest variety of literary genres than any other woman (and most men) during the century. Her works consisted of natural philosophy (natural science; the study of such fields as physics, chemistry, and biology), two volumes of plays, poetry, fantasies, essays, letters, a biography of her husband, and an autobiography. However, Cavendish is best known today for *The Description of a New World Called the Blazing World* (1666). It tells the story of a young lady who is abducted by a foreign merchant and taken by ship into another world, the Blazing World. After the merchant and the ships's crew become frozen during the passage into the new world, they thaw out and spread corruption. The woman is then transformed into an empress. Ruling over the Blazing World as a warrior queen, she puts down rebellions and commands armies of bird-men, worm-men, bear-men, and other war-

## Blazing World

Margaret Cavendish was the author of *The Description of a New World Called the Blazing World.* This novel gained the attention of twentieth-century scholars, who regard Cavendish as an unfairly neglected feminist writer. They argue that in *Blazing World* Cavendish presented a daring exploration of women's power.

*Blazing World* tells the story of a young lady who is abducted by a foreign merchant and taken by ship into another world (the Blazing World). The merchant and his crew become frozen during the passage into the new world, but soon they thaw out and spread corruption. The woman is then transformed into an empress to rule over the Blazing World as a warrior queen. The empress commands armies of bird-men, worm-men, bear-men, and other warriors to put down as series of rebellions. Following is an excerpt from *Blazing World* in which the Empress is sending in her armies to use water—which she has made flammable—to burn the towns of kings who did not meet her demands.

> ... before both the bird- and worm-men began their journey, the Empress commanded the bear-men to view through their telescopes what towns and cities those were that would not submit; and having a full information thereof, she instructed the bird- and bear-men what towns they should begin withal; in the meanwhile she sent to all the princes and sovereigns of those nations, to let them know that she would give them proof of her power, and check their obstinacies by burning some of their smaller towns,... At last ... the worm-men laid some fire-stones under the foundation of every house, and the bird-men placed some at the tops of them, so that both by rain and by some other moisture within the earth, the stones could not fail of burning. The bird-men in the meantime having learned some few words of their [the princes' and sovereigns'] language, told them, that the next time it did rain, their towns would be all on fire; at which they were amazed to hear men speak in the air; but withal they laughed when they heard them say that rain should fire their towns, knowing that the effect of water was to quench, not produce fire.

> At last a rain came, and upon a sudden all their houses appeared in a flaming fire, and the more water they poured on them, the more they did flame and burn; which struck such a fright and terror into all the neighbouring cities, nations and kingdoms, that for fear the like would happen to them, they and all the rest of the parts of the world granted the Empress's desire, and submitted to the monarch and sovereign of her native country, the King of ESFI; save one, which having seldom or never any rain, but only dews, which would soon be spent in a great fire, slighted her power;...

Source: Cavendish, Margaret. The Description of a New World Called the Blazing World and Other Writings, Kate Lilley, editor. New York: New York University Press, 1992, pp. 213–14.

riors in a series of fantastic adventures (see accompanying box). *Blazing World* is often called one of the first science fiction novels.

Cavendish associated with intellectuals and remained informed about the latest cultural developments. For instance, she dined with the French philosopher René Descartes (1596–1650) and she visited the all-male Royal Society, the prestigious scientific organization in London. Nevertheless, critics would not overlook her lack of formal training, since she knew no foreign languages and had no classical or scholarly education. Cavendish met with constant ridicule because she wrote so many works on so many different subjects. In fact, people thought she was insane and called her "Mad Madge." She also attracted negative attention by dressing unconventionally, often wearing a combination of women's and men's clothing.

Cavendish drew the greatest criticism for her work itself. She failed to produce polished writing, and she wrote in areas (such as science) where she could claim no expertise or education. Some regarded her as extremely arrogant for making her identity public. Others felt she was presumptuous for entering into debates with important thinkers such as Descartes. Those who acknowledged her contributions point to the originality of her writings and the many different subjects she wrote about. Some praised her for representing a scientific tradition outside of the male-dominated experimental method established by the philosopher and historian **Francis Bacon** (1561–1626; see entry). Cavendish was well known for her strong feminist views and the bold quality of her poetry. As a duchess she had advantages over middle-class authors, but the negative comments of her contemporaries—men and women alike—make clear that she lived in social isolation.

## Reputation reevaluated

Cavendish was a complex figure. While she was a staunch loyalist, she had few ties with the Anglican Church (the official religion of England). Moreover, she often published essays and letters that criticized England's social hierarchy and royal rule. She offered radical commentaries on women's social, political, intellectual, and legal standing. Despite her feminist ideals, her writing often painted women as weak, emotional creatures dependent upon the goodness and support of men. While others have seen her as privileged, she frequently portrayed herself as an intellectual and social outcast. She felt she had been isolated from the intellectual mainstream of universities and scholarly activity because she was a woman. Mistress of a remote estate, she seemed to be loved only by her husband. She found fulfillment in her study, however, and sought fame through her works despite her isolation. Cavendish continued to write and prepare her books for publication until her sudden death in 1673, at age fifty. While she may have been only a minor literary figure in the late 1600s, during the twentieth century her works gained serious attention from literary scholars, historians of science, women's historians, and those who study women philosophers.

## For Further Information

### Books

Cavendish, Margaret. *The Blazing World and Other Writings,* Kate Lilley, editor. New York: Penguin Classics, 1994.

### Web Sites

*Norton Topics Online: Van Schuppen, Engraving [portrait] of Margaret Cavendish.* [Online] Available http://www.wwnorton.com/nael/NTO/18thC/worlds/imcavendish.htm, April 4, 2002.

# Miguel de Cervantes

**1547
Alcalá de Henares, Spain
1616
Madrid, Spain**

**Novelist**

**T**he Spanish author Miguel de Cervantes Saavedra is famous for *Don Quixote,* (pronounced kee-HO-teh) considered one of the great masterpieces of world literature. This work was largely responsible for creating what is known as the modern novel. (A novel is a long written work that tells a story featuring fictional, or imaginary, characters involved in complex plots.) *Don Quixote* has been translated into more than sixty languages and its central character, Don Quixote of la Mancha, has become a major figure in Western culture. Don Quixote's image has been popularized in films, musicals, and paintings. His creator, known simply as Cervantes, lived at the end of the glorious years of the Spanish empire and fought heroically at the decisive sea battle of Lepanto. However, throughout his life Cervantes lived on the margins of society in a continuous struggle for survival. On occasion he was subjected to all the mishaps of Don Quixote, with extended periods in captivity and ceaseless economic hardship. These experiences are reflected in the novel's narrative, which is sympathetic and touchingly humane.

Miguel de Cervantes.

## Educates himself through reading

Cervantes was born in Alcalá de Henares, a village close to Madrid, Spain, in 1547. He was the fourth of seven children in the family of Rodrigo de Cervantes, a barber-surgeon, and Leonor de Cortina. His birth coincided with the final years of the powerful rule of the Holy Roman Emperor **Charles V** (1500–1558; see entry). Cervantes's father was continually oppressed by debts and barely made a living by moving from town to town. Little is known about Cervantes's education. He probably studied with the Jesuits (members of the religious order founded by **Ignatius of Loyola**; see entry), as he made references to them in some of his works. Evidence points to his having briefly studied in Madrid, Spain, in 1569, the same year his first poem appeared. He dedicated the poem to the recently deceased Elizabeth of Valois (1545–1568), the young wife of King Philip II (1527–1598; ruled 1556–98). It is known that Cervantes never attended university. Any knowledge he acquired over the years was due to his lifelong devotion to independent reading.

In 1570 Cervantes went to Italy and served in the household staff of Cardinal Giulio Acquaviva (1543–1615). During this time a man named Miguel de Cervantes had a scuffle with another man, Antonio de Segura, who was stabbed. An arrest warrant was issued for the accused stabber. It is uncertain if this Miguel de Cervantes was the same person who became a famous writer. It is known that Cervantes did leave Spain at this time and went to Italy. Those years in Italy were important to his intellectual development. He completed his education by reading Italian literature and philosophy. Italy was the capital of culture, and the Italian experience was central to Cervantes's development as an artist. Years later, in one of twelve stories in a collection titled *The Exemplary Novels,* Cervantes described the amazement of a young Spaniard as he faced the exuberant cities of sixteenth-century Italy for the first time. Throughout his life, Cervantes used his own experiences as literary inspiration.

## Wounded in battle

Later in 1570 Cervantes joined Diego de Urbina's Spanish forces at Naples. At that time Spain had the most powerful army in the world. Some of its bases were located in Italy for better access to the Mediterranean Sea, where Spain could fight the Ottoman Empire, which posed a major threat to European countries. The Spanish troops formed the most powerful army in Europe, feared by Spain's numerous enemies. Political alliances between European nations were fragile, so former enemies could quickly become friends, and vice-versa. The common enemy to all of Europe, however, was the Ottoman Empire, a vast Muslim (followers of the Islam religion) kingdom in Asia and parts of North Africa. The empire was based in Turkey. Fear of the Ottomans was especially great in Spain, where the Turkish citizen was identified with the Moor. (The Moors were originally nomadic people of the northern shores of Africa. They were mainly Berbers and Arabs, and strongly Muslim.) The Moors in Europe were the traditional foe of Catholics.

In 1492, after eight centuries of fighting, the Catholic monarchs King Ferdinand II of Aragon (1452–1516; ruled 1468–1516) and Isabella I of Castile (1451–1504; ruled 1479–1504) expelled the Moors from the Iberian Peninsula (name of the body of land where Spain and Portugal are located). Now the Turks threatened maritime traffic in the Mediterranean Sea with piracy (robbing of ships). On October 7, 1571, the Spanish Armada (fleet of heavily armed ships) faced the Turkish fleet in the Gulf of Lepanto, an inlet of the Ionian Sea extending into Corinth, Greece. Cervantes was aboard the ship *La Marquesa*. Although he was ill, he insisted on staying on deck during the confrontation. He fought heroically in the battle, suffering three wounds. The two in his chest healed, but his left hand was maimed and remained useless for the rest of his life. Cervantes took pride in these wounds and considered them a reminder of a great historical event. The Christian fleet won the Battle of Lepanto and earned the gratitude of the European nations threatened by the Turkish empire.

## Held captive by the Turks

After his wounds healed Cervantes remained in Italy as a soldier and participated in other campaigns (Navarino, Tunis, and La Galeta). Perhaps in order to obtain a promotion to the position of captain, he left Italy in 1575 to return to

Spain. On the way, three Turkish galleys (large ships powered by oars) intercepted his ship off the coast of Marseille, France. The ship was forced to surrender, and the crew and passengers were taken as captives to Algiers, Africa, a center of the North African Christian slave trade. Cervantes' brother, Rodrigo, was on the same boat and was his companion in captivity. Cervantes was carrying letters of commendation (recommendation) from high-ranking officials. This made him appear to be an important person. As a result, Cervantes's cruel captor, a Greek named Dali Mami, set his ransom (money paid in exchange for release of a captive) at an impossibly high price. For five fearful years Cervantes lived as a prisoner in harsh conditions. He made several failed escape attempts, and on two occasions other captives informed the Turks of his plans. The misconception that Cervantes was such an important person probably helped save him from being impaled (killed by being placed on a sharp stake) or tortured after he tried to escape.

In 1580, with the help of the Trinitarian friars, a Catholic religious order committed to the rescue of Christian captives, Cervantes's family finally managed to pay the five-hundred escudos (Spanish money) ransom that secured his freedom. Years later Cervantes described the experiences of Christian captives in several plays, as well as in the "Story of the Captive" a chapter in *Don Quixote*. In his first work of narrative prose, *Infomación de Argel* (Information of Algiers) Cervantes wrote about the four unsuccessful escape attempts he organized. The reader learns that he refused to inform on any of his fellow captives, and he described a near miraculous escape from the severe punishments usually given out for those offenses. Most of what is known about Cervantes's experience of captivity comes from this work, which shows fierce dedication to Christianity.

## Begins writing career

Cervantes's years of service in Italy and his subsequent years of captivity did not win him any privileges upon his return to Spain. He was not appointed to an official position, as he may have been expecting. Instead, he was briefly sent to Oran, Algeria, as a royal messenger in 1581. He struggled financially and tried to immigrate to the New World (European term for the Americas), but was denied official permission. During these years he wrote his first novel, *La Galatea* (1585). The novel gave him some prestige but not much economic help. In 1584 he married Catalina de Salazar y Palacios, a woman eighteen years his junior. She came into the marriage with a small dowry (money, goods, or estate that a woman brings to her husband in marriage), but little is known about their relationship. The previous year, Cervantes had fathered an illegitimate daughter with the wife of the owner of a tavern that was a meeting place for writers and comedians. Cervantes did not legally recognize this daughter, Isabel de Saavedra, who was his only offspring, until she was fifteen.

In 1587 the Spanish fleet entered Cervantes' life again, when he was appointed commissary (officer in charge of supplies) for the Spanish Armada. The Armada's mission was to diminish the British fleet, which posed a continuous threat to the Spanish galleons sailing back from America. Spain's decaying economy depended heavily on the timely arrival of the galleons with their precious cargo. Cervantes's position did not allow for a repeat of his previous heroic behavior. His duty was simply to acquire grain from rural communities. Not only did the Armada expedition end in a military catastrophe when it was defeated by the British navy in 1588, but Cervantes's assignment also brought him endless distress. When municipalities and local churches refused to pay, he was accused of mismanagement. As a result, he was imprisoned in Córdoba in 1592 and Seville in 1597. It was probably during his last imprisonment that he conceived the idea of writing *Don Quixote*.

Although Cervantes published *The Exemplary Novels* in 1612, he had written them during the 1590s. In the prologue (introduction) Cervantes declared himself the first person ever to write novellas (a form of short fictitious stories originating in Italy) in Spanish. The story "El coloquio de los perros" (Colloquy of Dogs) follows the conversation of two dogs. "La española inglesa" (The Anglo-Spanish Lady) recounts the romantic adventure of a young girl who is kidnapped. She is taken to England where she keeps her Catholic faith and falls in love with the son of her captor. The main character in "El Licenciado Vidriera" (The Glass Licentiate) is much like the madman in *Don Quixote*: a scholar who becomes insane and believes that he is made out of brittle glass.

## Cervantes, the Failed Playwright

Cervantes tried without success to become a playwright. In Madrid, theater-going had become a very popular form of entertainment, much like going to the movies today. There were several open-air theaters in the city, and the people were eager to see new plays. Cervantes decided to try his fortune in the thriving market of comedies. He wrote several plays, but only two have survived from this period: *El cerco de Numancia* (The siege of Numantia) and *El trato de Argel* (The business of Algiers.) Cervantes's theatrical attempts were not very successful. Cervantes's competition was the public's favorite playwright Lope de Vega (1562–1635), a prolific writer who claimed the ability to write a play in one evening. Cervantes tried to establish a national theater based on the Greek and Roman model, which consisted of four acts, with comedies and tragedies clearly separated. Vega was more successful because he formed what is known as *comedia.* Comedia is divided into three acts, with no distinction between comedy and tragedy, and filled with fierce patriotism and celebration of national values. Cervantes did not abandon the theater altogether, however. In 1615, at a bookseller's request, Cervantes collected some of his plays and published them under the title of *Ocho comedias y ocho entremeses nunca representados* (Eight plays and eight interludes never performed). The plays were published in the three-act *comedia* form, with the interludes (short plays between acts of longer plays) in the traditional form of farce (obvious humor). These plays were never performed in Cervantes's lifetime.

His temporary insanity gives him remarkable understanding of the problems of his society.

## *Don Quixote* is a great success

In 1605 Cervantes published the first part of *Don Quixote*. It was his first literary success and established him, at age fifty-eight, as an important writer. The novel contains a number of the popular literary styles and subjects of the time, such as the romantic novel focusing on tales of chivalry, and issues of religion and faith. (Chivalry was a medieval tradition that required knights, or nobleman soldiers, to pledge themselves to a complex code of honor. Knights frequently dedicated their military adventures to ladies, whose virtue they vowed to protect.) Cervantes originally intended to

EL INGENIOSO
HIDALGO DON QVI-
XOTE DE LA MANCHA,

*Compuesto por Miguel de Ceruantes
Saauedra.*

DIRIGIDO AL DVQVE DE BEIAR,
Marques de Gibraleon, Conde de Benalcaçar, y Baña-
res, Vizconde de la Puebla de Alcozer, Señor de
las villas de Capilla, Curiel, y
Burguilios.

Año,                                                     1605.

CON PRIVILEGIO,
*EN MADRID*, Por Iuan de la Cuesta.

Véndese en casa de Francisco de Robles, librero del Rey nro señor.

mock the popular chivalric romances and the adventures stories of errant (traveling) knights. He created Don Quixote, an
elderly gentleman who becomes insane due to his excessive
passion for reading chivalric romances. Don Quixote leaves
his home, having decided to revive heroic times by reenact-
ing knightly feats. Later, with the promise of fabulous re-
wards, he convinces the poor peasant, Sancho Panza, to be
his squire (shield bearer). The novel narrates in a descriptive

and majestic manner the absurd adventures of knight and squire as they travel through Spain. Cervantes depicts characters who reflected their society, thus making a commentary on the social customs of the day. The book was an immediate success and was reedited several times in subsequent years. It was translated into English as early as 1612 and eventually appeared in French and other European languages.

The success of *Don Quixote* was so extraordinary that in 1614 a man named Avellaneda attempted to write a sequel without the permission of Cervantes. This unauthorized work so enraged Cervantes that he decided to write the second part of *Don Quixote,* which was successfully published in 1615. This continuation is considered to be as good as, if not better than, the first installment. The second part is more reflective and possesses greater structural unity. At the conclusion Don Quixote dies after recovering his sanity, much to the distress of a transformed Sancho who is eager to engage in more adventures. With Don Quixote's death Cervantes ended the possibility of further adventures for his character.

*Don Quixote* is still widely read in nearly every language throughout the world. According to the web site *Famous Hispanics* The novel contributed many familiar expressions to the English language: "the sky"s the limit," "thanks for nothing," "mind your own business," "think before you speak," "forgive and forget," "to smell a rat," "turning over a new leaf," "the haves and have-nots," "born with a silver spoon in his mouth," "the pot calling the kettle black," and "you've seen nothing yet." *Don Quixote* also contains one of the most memorable scenes in world literature: in Chapter Eight, Don Quixote—against the common-sense warnings of Sancho Panza—charges windmills that he mistakenly believes to be evil giants (see accompanying box). This scene resulted in the expression "tilting at windmills," which is used to describe a foolhardy venture that is sure to end in failure or disappointment.

## Novel becomes classic

Writers in Cervantes's time lost the economic rights to their work after selling it to a merchant. Therefore, Cervantes's success did not grant him the economic security that

## Windmills In His Head

*Don Quixote* contains one of the most memorable scenes in world literature: Against the warnings of his squire Sancho Panza, the errant knight Don Quixote (spelled Quijote here) charges windmills that he mistakenly believes to be evil giants. Following are excerpts from the windmill scene.

*Just then, they [Don Quixote and Sancho Panza] came upon thirty or forty windmills ... and as soon as Don Quijote saw them he said to his squire:*

*"Destiny guides our fortunes more favorably than we could have expected. Look here, Sancho Panza, my friend, and see those thirty or so wild giants, with whom I intend to do battle and to kill each and all of them, so with their stolen booty we can begin to enrich ourselves. This is noble, righteous warfare, for it is wonderfully useful to God to have such an evil race wiped from the face of the earth."*

*"What giants?" asked Sancho Panza.*

*"The ones you can see over there," answered his master, " with the huge arms, some of which are very nearly two leagues long."*

*"Now look, your grace," said Sancho, " what you see over there aren't giants, but windmills, and what seem to be arms are just their sails, that go around in the wind and turn the millstone."*

*"Obviously," replied Don Quijote, "you don't know much about adventures.*

best-sellers bring their authors today. Cervantes's chief literary achievements came late in his life. His widow published his last book, *Los trabajos de Persiles y Segismunda* (The Labors of Persiles and Segismunda) after his death. Cervantes thought that its success would exceed that of *Don Quixote*, but it did not. Cervantes signed the dedication of the book to the Count of Lemos on April 19, 1616. He died four days later and was buried in an unmarked grave in the Trinitarians' convent in Madrid. His wife survived him by ten years, and his daughter Isabel de Saavedra died in 1662.

All of Cervantes's major works have been translated into English, and *Don Quixote* is one of the few books translated into most languages. The literary influence of the novel has been immense. Direct traces can be identified in the work of countless other authors of various nationalities. In addition, thinkers and philosophers have dedicated essays to the myth of Don Quixote. Twentieth-century musical productions, such as *The Man of La Mancha,* and movies have been

*Those are giants—and if you're frightened, take yourself away from here and say your prayers, while I go charging into savage and unequal combat with them."*

*Saying which, he spurred his horse, Rocinante, paying no attention to the shouts of Sancho Panza ... but charged on, crying:*

*"Flee not, oh cowards and dastardly creatures, for he who attacks you is a knight alone and unaccompanied."*

When Don Quixote and Rocinante reach the first windmill, a sudden gust of wind starts it moving. The sail breaks the knight's shield and spear, knocking him and his horse to the ground. Sancho comes to their rescue on his donkey, exclaiming, "God help me!... Didn't I tell your grace to be careful what you did, that these were just windmills, and anyone who could ignore that had to have windmills in his head?" Don Quixote is determined not to listen to common sense, however, and he replies, "Silence, Sancho, my friend.... Even more than other things, war is subject to perpetual change." Then he mounts Rocinante, and the knight and his squire set out for further adventures.

*Source: Cervantes, Miguel de. Don Quijote. Burton Raffel, translator, and Diana de Armas Wilson, editor. New York: Norton, 1999, pp. 43–44.*

inspired by *Don Quixote*. Modern artists like the Spanish painter Pablo Picasso (1881–1973) have immortalized the image of the errant knight escorted by his faithful squire.

## For More Information

### Books

Canavaggio, Jean. *Cervantes.* J. R. Jones, translator. New York: Norton, 1990.

Cervantes, Miguel de. *Adventures of Don Quixote.* J. M. Cohen, translator. New York: Penguin, 1988.

### Sound Recordings

Cervantes, Miguel de. *Don Quixote.* St. Paul, Minn.: HighBridge,1997.

*Man of La Mancha.* New York: Sony Classical, 1996.

### Video Recordings

*Don Quixote.* TNT Original: Hallmark Entertainment Production, 2000.

*Man of La Mancha.* Farmington Hills, Mich.: CBS/FOX Video, 1984.

### Web sites

"Cervantes, Miguel de." *Britannica.com.* [Online] Available http://www.britannica.com/eb/article?eu=114980&tocid=0&query=cervantes, April 5, 2002.

"Cervantes Saavedra, Miguel de." *Encyclopedia.com.* [Online] Available http://www.encyclopedia.com/searchpool.asp?target=@DOCTITLE%20Cervantes%20Saavedra%20%20Miguel%20de, April 5, 2002.

*The Don Quixote Exhibit.* [Online] Available http://milton.mse.jhu.edu:8006/, April 5, 2002.

"Miguel de Cervantes Saavedra." *Famous Hispanics.* [Online] Available http://coloquio.com/famosos/cervante.html, April 5, 2002.

# Charles V (also known as Charles I)

**February 24, 1500,
Ghent, the Netherlands
September 21, 1558
San Jeronimo de Yuste, Spain**

**Holy Roman Emperor and king of Spain**

"Therefore I am determined to pledge for this cause all my realms, my friends, my body, my life and my soul ... to defend the Catholic Faith."

*Charles V.*

**Charles V.** *©Gianni Dagli Orti/Corbis. Reproduced by permission of Corbis Corporation.*

During his reign as Holy Roman Emperor and king of Spain, Charles V became the ruler of one of the largest empires in world history. A member of the powerful Habsburg family based in Austria and Spain, he inherited far-reaching territories: the ancestral Habsburg family estates; the Spanish Empire; the kingdoms of Germany, Hungary, Bohemia, Naples, and Sicily; the duchy of Milan; the Netherlands; and possessions in North Africa and the Americas. His empire was so vast that he owned roughly twice the amount of land as the king of France. Charles V dominated the stage of European and world politics from 1516 until his death in 1558. A man of enormous military talent, he endeared himself to his soldiers, and eventually even his Spanish subjects, by his courage and love of action. Next to him, **Francis I**, the king of France (1494–1547; see entry), and **Henry VIII** (1491–1547; see entry), the king of England, were but minor players on the political chessboard of Europe.

## A teen-age ruler

Charles was born in Ghent, Netherlands, in 1500 to Philip I (the Handsome) (1478–1506), archduke of Austria, and Joanna (called the Mad; 1479–1555) of Castile—a province of Spain and seat of the empire. Charles was the heir to a glittering collection of European titles and lands. His maternal grandparents were King Ferdinand II (1452–1516; ruled 1468–1516) of Castile and Queen Isabella I (1451–1504; ruled 1474–1504) of Aragon. His paternal grandparents were Holy Roman Emperor Maximilian I (1459–1519; ruled 1493–1519) and Mary of Burgundy (1457–1482). When Charles was only six, his father died. Joanna suffered from mental problems, which grew worse after Philip's death, and forced her to remain in her native land of Castile. Charles, along with three of his sisters, was transported to the household of his paternal aunt, Margaret of Austria (1480–1530), in the Netherlands. Charles spent his early years guided by two mentors, Margaret and his chamberlain (bedchamber attendant), Guillaume de Croy, the sieur de Chievres. The prince's guardians also assigned a priest, Adrian Florensz Boeyens (Adrian of Utrecht; 1459–1523), to serve as his spiritual guide. Adrian later become Pope Adrian VI (reigned 1522–23). Charles enjoyed hunting, music, singing, art, and architecture, but he despised learning Latin, Greek, or any other ancient language.

When his father died Charles inherited the Burgundian lands of the Netherlands and Franche-Comté. At the age of fifteen he became ruler of the Netherlands. In 1516, upon the death of his grandfather Ferdinand II, he inherited Spain and its vast empire. A year later, when he visited Castile, the immature monarch brought with him a group of Flemish advisers, which caused much resentment among the Castilians. They felt the Flemish advisers would promote the interests of the Habsburgs in the Netherlands over the welfare of the king's Spanish subjects. Although he stayed in Spain until 1520, he was young, unsure of himself, and utterly unfamiliar with the language or customs of his proud Spanish subjects. Spain, and especially the province of Castile, however, remained the heart of his far-reaching realm for the remainder of his life.

## A young king, a growing empire

When his other grandfather, Maximilian, died in 1519, Charles bid for the vacant throne of the Holy Roman

Empire, which his Habsburg ancestors had ruled for centuries. Although Francis I of France and Henry VIII of England were also vying for the position, Charles was able to count on vast sums in bribe money. A loan of 850,000 florins, or European gold coins, had been secured as bribe money from the wealthy Jacob Fugger (1459–1525), head of a banking syndicate in Germany. (Some historians put the figure closer to 500,000 florins.) Military blackmail was also used to sway the electors (noblemen appointed to select an emperor). In June 1519 Charles was unanimously elected emperor, but he was not officially crowned by the pope until 1530 when the hostilities between Charles and the pope had ended. The rivalry initiated among Charles, Francis I, and Henry VIII was to last for the balance of the young kings' natural lives.

During this time Mercurino Gattinara, Charles's grand chancellor (chief secretary), had told Charles that God had set him on the path to world monarchy. Gattinara also said that he who sat on the imperial throne was the leader of all Christendom (Roman Catholic Europe), ordained by God himself. There is no doubt that Charles had come to see himself as the defender of Christianity against Islam in the Ottoman Empire to the east and, later, Protestants in Germany. This exalted role did not sit well with many of Charles's Spanish subjects, however, who believed that he ought to be spending his time and efforts on the throne of Spain. In 1520, Castile erupted in the Revolt of the Comuneros over resentment of the Flemish influence at Charles's court.

Juan de Padilla (c. 1490–1521), a representative from Toledo, Spain, had organized leaders in other cities into a "Holy League of Cities." Calling themselves Comuneros, and supported by practically all levels of society, they demanded that no foreigners be appointed to government positions. They also declared that Spain's foreign policy must promote Spanish interests. Charles learned that they resented him for leaving the country so early to seek the German title of Holy Roman Emperor (he had been in Spain for only three years) and for the financial burdens he had levied on them. Charles had left Adrian behind as Spanish regent, (one who rules in place of a minor or an absent monarch) but the uprising required the personal attention of Charles. Upon his return from Germany in 1522, Charles brutally crushed the rebellion and executed more than 270 people. From that time on he was regarded mainly as a "Spanish king," and the people of Spain adopted him with an uncompromising affection.

When Spain was once more at peace, Charles faced two immediate challenges: the growing Lutheran movement and the threat from France to his possessions in Italy. Charles addressed the Lutheran problem by supporting the doctrines of the Roman Catholic Church but allowing for reform, as long as it was done without heresy (violation of the laws of God and the church). He believed it was his job to evaluate whether or not religious reform was heretical. This was Charles's intent when he called the German reformer **Martin Luther** (1483–1546; see entry) to defend his religious positions at the Diet of Worms in 1521 (see accompanying box). Luther was a German monk who had sparked the reform movement in 1517 when he presented his *Ninety-Five Theses,* a list of grievances against the Catholic Church, at Wittenberg, Germany.

## Spain at war with France

Charles's other problem was the Spanish war with France in Italy. Called the Italian Wars (1494–1559), this conflict involved a dispute between France and Spain over territory in Italy. Spain and France had a long history of warring with one another, most recently over the rich and divided Italian principalities. An early key battle came in 1499, when Ferdinand II of Aragon had defeated Louis XII of France (1462–1515; ruled 1498–1515). Spain had established a reputation for an invincible infantry (soldiers trained to fight in the front line of battle). In fact, Spain's famed land troops did not lose a pitched battle for 150 years. Francis I, however, threatened Italy. In 1515 he had triumphantly defeated Massimiliano Sforza (1493–1530; ruled 1512–15), duke of Milan, at the Battle of Marignano. Pope Leo X (1475–1521; reigned 1513–21) and Charles V came to the aid of Sforza. The result was the tremendous victory of Spanish forces over the French at Pavia in 1525. Francis was humiliated when he was captured and removed to Madrid as a prisoner for more than a year. In 1526 he agreed to leave his two sons as hostages and married Eleanor, Charles's sister and the dowager queen of Portugal. Once he was safely home, Francis rejected the terms

# Emperor Confronts Reformer

When Holy Roman Emperor Charles V was only seventeen, an obscure German monk named Martin Luther presented his *Ninety-Five Theses* at a Catholic church in Wittenberg, Germany. In a now-famous attack, Luther listed his grievances with Roman Catholicism and initiated the Protestant Reformation in Europe. Among other issues, Luther attacked the church practice of selling indulgences (forgiveness of sins) in order to finance the construction of Saint Peter's Basilica, the main Catholic church, in Rome. The reformer also criticized the corruption of the clergy and challenged traditional interpretations of scripture (text of the Bible, the Christian holy book). Luther's charges caused considerable controversy, pitting the pope and clergy as well as kings, noblemen, and common people against one another. Charles was preoccupied with his bitterly fought election as emperor and with the Comuneros' revolt in Spain, so he dismissed Luther as an insignificant heretic. This was a mistake. During the crucial years of 1517 to 1521, the Lutheran movement gained much momentum, especially in Germany and the Netherlands.

Finally, in 1521 Charles summoned Luther before the Imperial Diet (conference of representatives of the Holy Roman Empire) at Worms, Germany, to explain himself. In an epic face-to-face confrontation with the emperor, the German priest refused to budge on his controversial views. Charles, in turn, rejected Luther's doctrine and thereafter considered him a heretic beyond the scope of rehabilitation. Declaring Luther an "outlaw of the church," Charles accused Luther of having misguided ideas and single-handedly trying to overturn Christian teachings, which had existed for a thousand years. The emperor vowed that he would do everything in his power to defend the Catholic religion.

of the treaty he had signed in Madrid, and ransomed his sons for two million florins. Thus the war between Spain and France continued to rage in Italy.

Elsewhere in Europe, Charles was being threatened on yet another front by **Süleyman I** (1494–1566; see entry), sultan of the Ottoman Empire, a vast Muslim kingdom in Asia and parts of North Africa. Süleyman challenged Charles's authority in the area around the Mediterranean Sea as well as the Habsburg possessions in central Europe. In 1526 King Louis II of Hungary and Bohemia (1506–1526; ruled 1516–26) died at the Battle of Mohacs in Hungary, and Charles inherit-

An engraving of the Battle of Pavia in 1525 between the forces of Francis I and Charles V. Charles and his troops won a tremendous victory over the French.
*Reproduced by permission of Hulton Archive.*

ed these thrones. Charles married Isabella of Portugal in the same year. The emperor was then confronted with more problems in Italy, when Pope Clement VII (1478–1534; reigned 1523–34) joined Francis I and Henry VIII in the League of Cognac to oppose Charles's attempts to expand his empire. Charles's Spanish and German troops stationed in Rome, angered by repeated delays in the payment of their wages, brutally sacked the holy city in 1527. This action demonstrated the massive power at Charles's disposal and the limited ability of sixteenth-century monarchs to fully control their soldiers. Clement, who had been locked away in a tower for his own safety, was horrified and quickly came to terms with Charles, as did Henry. Deserted by his allies, Francis was also forced to make peace by 1529. When the Turks (another name for the Ottomans) continued to menace Europe, most of Christendom's desperate rulers turned to Charles V for protection. In 1529, and again three years later, Charles's imperial forces united with armies headed by his brother, Ferdinand I (1503–1546), to defeat the Turks.

## Hailed hero of Christendom

With their hostilities behind them, Clement VII officially crowned Charles as Holy Roman Emperor at Bologna, Italy, in 1530. Negotiations continued between the emperor and those of his subjects who had embraced the Protestant faith, but no headway was made. In 1535 Charles became the hero of all Christendom when he triumphantly captured a Turkish stronghold at Tunis (now Tunisia, Africa) and liberated thousands of Christians who had been held prisoner by the Turks. A year later he appeared before the college of cardinals (a committee of church officials, ranking directly below the pope, who elect the pope) and Pope Paul III (1468–1549; reigned 1534–49) in Rome to challenge Francis I. Charles thought the two should decide the fate of Italy through personal combat. Francis, who fancied himself a chivalrous knight throughout his entire reign, abruptly refused. Charles then invaded Provence, France, but operations quickly bogged down. Paul III interceded and brought about a temporary truce in 1538. That same year Charles rushed to Ghent, Netherlands, to quash a rebellion of local elites under the rule of his sister, Mary of Hungary (1505–1558). Again the emperor exhibited little tolerance for challenges to his authority as he executed thirteen of the rebels. Three years later Charles suffered a major disappointment when a large-scale amphibious (land and water) assault on the Ottoman base of Algiers, Africa, had to be aborted due to inclement weather.

In 1542 Charles struggled over the question of whether to renounce his claim to Milan, Italy, in the interest of peace with Francis I, or to give the duchy to his son **Philip II** (1527–1598; see entry). In the end he decided on Philip, and a fresh war between the German house of Habsburg and the French house of Valois began. Charles defeated the French king and then agreed to terms. Finally in 1543 Paul III convened the long-awaited Council of Trent to reform the Roman Catholic Church from within. The council ended with a basic reaffirmation of Catholic doctrine, but with a decidedly more tolerant tone. Despite the compromise, the troubles between Protestants and Catholics in Europe were only in their infancy. Charles's enemies, the German Protestant princes, sought collective protection from Spanish power by banding together in an elaborate alliance known as the Schmalkaldic League.

Charles would not stand for any alliance aimed at limiting his kingdom.

In 1547 Charles won perhaps his greatest victory. Seventy thousand imperial soldiers annihilated the forces of the German Protestant princes at Mühlberg, Germany. Although hostilities ended for a time, by 1551 the German princes had found another ally in the new king of France, Henry II (1519–1559; ruled 1547–59). Efforts to defeat Charles became more intense. One German elector even came dangerously close to capturing the emperor himself. After the Battle of Mühlberg, Charles V concentrated more on foreign policy through marriage than through war. In 1554 he engineered a shaky Spanish-English alliance by arranging a marriage between his son Philip II to the Catholic English queen, Mary Tudor (1516–1558; ruled 1553–58). England reluctantly agreed to the marriage, but Parliament (main ruling body of Great Britain) would ultimately refuse to recognize Philip as an independent monarch. When no heirs were born by the time of Mary's death in 1558, all of the emperor's work was for nothing.

## Patron and retiree

Throughout his reign Charles was a great lover of the arts, especially music. He ruled at the height of the Renaissance, a cultural revolution that began in Italy in the mid-1300s. The Renaissance was initiated by scholars called humanists who promoted the human-centered values of ancient Greece and Rome. Humanist ideals were soon influencing the arts, literature, philosophy, science, religion, and politics in Italy. During the early fifteenth century, innovations of the Italian Renaissance began spreading into the rest of Europe and reached a peak in the sixteenth century. Like all Renaissance monarchs, Charles sought to enhance his power by being a generous patron of the arts. Yet he was not the easiest of patrons to please. He took his famous chapel singers with him when he traveled and even kept them by him after he abdicated, or left, the throne. The groups's fame helped maintain the reputation of Flemish music for the rest of the sixteenth century. Charles also built a chapel for his wife and gave his son Philip, when he reached the age of twelve, a suite of musicians that included singers, instrumentalists, and composers.

## Conquistadors Expand Spanish Empire

As Charles was expanding his empire in Europe, Spanish explorers were extending his reach into the New World (the European term for the Americas). Spanish conquest had begun in 1492, during the reign of the Catholic monarchs—and Charles's grandparents—King Ferdinand II of Castile and Queen Isabella I of Aragon. Ferdinand and Isabella commissioned the Italian navigator Christopher Columbus (1451–1506) to take his now-famous voyage in search of a more direct route to Asia. After Columbus's ships went off course in the Atlantic Ocean, he "discovered" islands (present-day Watling Island, Cuba, and Haiti) in the ocean off the continent of North America. This "new world" was claimed for Spain in the name of Ferdinand and Isabella.

In 1521, during Charles's reign, conquistadors (conquerors) went onto the mainland of North America. Hernán Cortés (1485–1547), a young and handsome noble lawyer from Spain, led a group of six hundred Spanish adventurers against the immense Aztec Empire in Mexico. Ignoring an order from Cuba's Spanish governor Diego Velázquez not to sail, Cortés spurred his men forward by burning their ships (which was their only route of escape) once they had landed on the Yucatán peninsula. Velázquez was trying to prevent Cortés from leading an independent expedition to the Yucataán. Cortés set sail anyway, and he burned his ships to prevent any Velázquez sympathizers from returning to Cuba. Cortés's astounding feat of defeating the Aztecs won tremendous lands and wealth for his Spanish sovereign. This was not the only help Charles received from the conquistadors. Francisco Pizarro (1475–1541), a former indentured servant, won a spectacular victory when he conquered the fabled Inca Empire in 1533. Landing on the Pacific coast of Peru with just 2 cannons, 37 horses, and 180 men, Pizarro accomplished one of the most incredible coups (violent overthrow of a government) of all time. The enormous wealth of the Incas was to fuel Spanish foreign policy well into the seventeenth century.

Charles so admired the work of the famous Italian Renaissance painter Titian that he gave Titian the title Count Palatine. He summoned the painter to Augsburg in 1548, where Titan produced one of his most famous portraits, *Charles V at the Battle of Mühlberg.* In this painting Charles is depicted as a triumphant knight. In 1548 Titian painted a portrait of the seated emperor and in 1554 he began the *Gloria,* which depicts a kneeling Charles and his wife among a group of people, all adoring the Trinity (God the Father,

Christ the Son, and the Holy Spirit) and the Virgin Mary. Charles also had other favorite painters and poets who enjoyed his patronage. Among them were the Spanish poet Garcilaso de la Vega, the Italian sculptor Leone Leoni and Leoni's son Pompeo Leoni.

By 1555 Charles was seriously considering abdication and retirement. He was unwilling to accept the religious peace his brother Ferdinand had secured between the Catholics and Protestants. The principle of *cuius regio eius religio* (whose the reign, his the religion) not only left Charles angry and frustrated, but made him ineffective as a leader. Philip was of sufficient age and maturity to rule, and the enormous strain of directing such a massive empire had clearly taken its toll on Charles. The empire was more than solid. In America the Spaniards had established courts of law in eight colonies and had founded three universities. Tons of silver from the mines of Potosi, Bolivia, along with Mexican and Peruvian gold and gems were streaming into Spanish ports aboard giant galleons (ships). Charles had firmly consolidated the Spanish hold on an area that contained one-fifth of the world's population. Satisfied that he had accomplished his goals, in January 1556 Charles V abdicated the bulk of his vast possessions to Philip II. Charles then retired to a monastery at San Jeronimo de Yuste in Spain. He bestowed the prestigious title of Holy Roman Emperor and the traditional Habsburg feudal properties on his younger brother, Ferdinand I. On September 21, 1558, clutching a crucifix, Charles V died in Spain.

## Charles's legacy

Although some scholars have pointed to the events of his last years as signs of failure on Charles's part, such a position is hardly justifiable. He ruled vast and widespread territories for forty years, adding immensely to his possessions by unparalleled successes in the New World. He kept Spain at the pinnacle of world power, a position it did not relinquish for one hundred years. Although Charles's efforts against the Turks were not completed, he had preserved Christendom far better than any of his peers. He was a dedicated fighter for the cause of Catholicism. Through his memorable victories at

Pavia and Mühlberg, he thoroughly dominated Francis I and Henry VIII. Charles's later years, spent largely as an adviser to Philip, were not in vain. Just one year before Charles died, Philip decisively ended more than a half century of Habsburg-Valois conflict over Italy by demolishing the French at Saint Quentin. At Cateau-Cambrésis in 1559 he signed a peace treaty that preserved Spain's preeminence in Europe. In 1571 one of Charles's other sons, John of Austria (1547–1578), settled old Habsburg accounts by crushing the Turks in one of the world's great naval battles at the Gulf of Lepanto (now called Gulf of Corinth).

## For More Information

### Books

McGuigan, Dorothy Gies. *The Habsburgs*. Garden City, N.Y.: Doubleday, 1966.

Rady, Martyn. *The Emperor Charles V*. New York: Longman, 1988.

*Young Charles V, 1500–1531*. Alain Saint-Saëns, editor. New Orleans: University Press of the South, 2000.

### Web Sites

"Charles V, Holy Roman Emperor." *The Columbia Encyclopedia*. [Online] Available http://www.bartleby.com/65/ch/Charles5HRE.html, April 5, 2002.

# Nicolaus Copernicus

**February 19, 1473**
**Toruń, Poland**
**May 24, 1543**
**Formbork, Poland**

**Theologian and astronomer**

**Nicolaus Copernicus.**
*Photograph courtesy of The Library of Congress.*

The Polish theologian and astronomer Nicolaus Copernicus (1473–1543) is credited with starting the scientific revolution in 1543 by publishing *De revolutionibus orbium coelestium* (On the revolutions of the heavenly orbs). In this work he proposed that the Sun, not the Earth, is the center of the universe. Although the book received little attention at the time, Copernicus's theory later caused considerable controversy. Not only did it contradict the accepted ideas of ancient astronomers, but it also challenged the teachings of the Roman Catholic Church. In the early 1600s the Italian astronomer **Gailileo** (1564–1642; see entry) used Copernicus's observations to formulate his own proof of a Sun-centered universe, unleashing a confrontation with the church that lasted into the late twentieth century.

## Pursues interest in astronomy

Nicolaus Copernicus had a life-long career as a canon (clergyman at a cathedral) in the Roman Catholic Church, pursuing the study of astronomy (the study of celestial bodies, such as planets, stars, the Sun, and the Moon) in his spare time. He was born on February 19, 1473, in Toruń, Poland, about one hundred miles south of Danzig (now Gdańsk). He belonged to a family of merchants. His uncle, the bishop and ruler of Ermland, Poland, was the person to whom Copernicus owed his education, career, and security. Copernicus graduated from the University of Cracow in Poland 1494. Although he did not attend any classes in astronomy, he began to collect books on astronomy and mathematics during his student years. In 1496 Copernicus set out for Bologna, Italy, to study canon (church) law. In Bologna, he came under the influence of the astronomer Domenico Maria de Novara (1454–1504) and recorded the positions of some planets. He did the same in Rome, where he spent the Jubilee Year of 1500. (Jubilee is a time of special solemnity declared by the pope, head of the Roman Catholic Church, every twenty-five years.)

In 1501 Copernicus made a brief visit to Frauenburg. His first official act as canon was to apply for permission to spend three more years in Italy, which was granted him on his promise that he would study medicine. Copernicus settled in Padua, but later he moved to the University of Ferrara, where he obtained the degree of doctor in canon law in 1503. Only then did he take up the study of medicine in Padua, prolonging his leave of absence until 1506. Upon returning to Ermland, Copernicus stayed in his uncle's castle at Heilsberg as his personal physician and secretary. During that time he translated from Greek into Latin the eighty-five poems of the seventh-century Byzantine poet Theophylactus Simacattes (died after 640). The work was printed in Cracow in 1509.

## Formulates controversial theory

At this time Copernicus was also mulling over the problems of astronomy, especially the heliocentric (Sun-centered) system. He outlined the system in a short unpublished manuscript known as the *Commentariolus* (Small commentary), which he completed around 1512. Copernicus himself referred to this work as "Sketch of Hypotheses Made by Nicolaus Copernicus on the Heavenly Motions." Copies of the manuscript circulated among his friends, who were eager to know about his ideas. At the outset of *Commentariolus,* Copernicus listed seven axioms (statements accepted as being true), each of which stated a feature of the heliocentric system. The third and most controversial axiom stated that since all planets revolve on orbits around the Sun, the Sun must therefore be the center of the universe. This idea was controversial because astronomers at the time accepted the theory of the ancient Egyptian scholar Ptolemy (also known as Claudius Ptolemaeus; c. A.D. 100–c. 170), who concluded that the Sun revolved around the Earth.

Ptolemy presented his views on the heavens in the *Almagest,* which covered all aspects of mathematical astronomy (study of heavenly bodies through mathematical calculations) as it was understood in antiquity. To attain knowledge of the universe, Ptolemy argued, one must study astronomy because it leads to the Prime Mover (God), the first cause of all heavenly motions. Ptolemy followed earlier Greek thinkers such as Aristotle (384–322 B.C.), who believed that the Earth is the center of a fixed and perfectly balanced universe. Ptolemy argued that the universe has a spherical (round) shape and that stars and planets move in circular patterns. He also contended that the Earth is spherical and remains in a fixed position at the center of the universe. However, the Earth's size is insignificant in comparison to that of the heavens. According to Ptolemy, all heavenly bodies rotated around the Earth in larger and larger circles that shared approximately the same center point. The order of the circles was, first, the Moon, then Mercury, Venus, the Sun, Mars, Jupiter, Saturn, and the last sphere of the fixed stars. Ptolemy's view was enforced by the Catholic Church, which found supporting evidence in the Bible (the Christian holy book).

In *Commentariolus* Copernicus proposed a system in which the Sun replaced the Earth at the center of the universe, and the Earth was moved to take the place of the vacated Sun. Copernicus stated that the heavens (planets and stars) do not actually rotate. They only appear to do so because the Earth makes a daily rotation on its own axis (an imaginary line that extends through the center of the globe from north to south). Similarly, the Sun appears to rotate along a path around the Earth only because the Earth makes an annual rotation around the Sun. The motions of the planets are also merely reflections of the Earth's travel in its orbit.

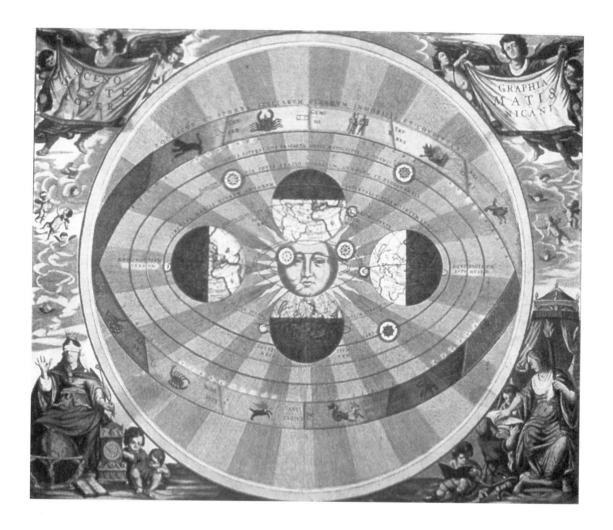

## Turns astronomy "upside down"

*Commentariolus* produced no reaction, either in print or in letters, but Copernicus's fame began to spread. In 1514 he received an invitation to be present as an astronomer at the Fifth Lateran Council in Rome, a church conference that had as one of its aims the reform of the calendar. He did not attend. His secretiveness only seemed to enhance his reputation. In 1522 the secretary to the king of Poland asked Copernicus to give an opinion on *De motu octavae spherae* (On the motion of the eighth sphere), which had just been published by Johann Werner, a respected mathematician. This time Copernicus responded in a letter expressing a rather low regard for Werner's work. Copernicus also stated that he was

An illustration of Nicolaus Copernicus's controversial theory that the Earth revolves around the Sun and not the other way around as proposed by Ptolemy. *©Bettmann/Corbis. Reproduced by permission of Corbis Corporation.*

writing his own study on the motion of the stars. He could pursue his scientific work only in his spare time, however, because his responsibilities as a canon kept him busy. He was involved in various aspects of the church, including legal and medical matters, but especially administrative and financial functions. In fact, he composed a booklet in 1522 on the remedies of inflation (increase in prices), which then largely meant the preservation of the same amount of gold and silver in coins. Although Copernicus did not publish anything about astronomy and had no contact with other astronomers, rumors continued to circulate about the revolutionary nature of his heliocentric theory.

Not all the comments were flattering. The Protestant reformer **Martin Luther** (1483–1546; see entry) denounced Copernicus for foolishly trying to overturn established theories of astronomy. In 1531 a satirical play was produced about Copernicus in Elbing, Prussia, by a local schoolmaster. In Rome things went better. In 1533 John Widmanstad, a secretary of the pope, lectured on Copernicus's theory before Pope Clement VII (1478–1534; reigned 1523–34) and several cardinals (church officials who rank directly below the pope). Three years later Cardinal Nikolaus von Schönberg wrote Copernicus a letter, urging him to publish his thoughts. It was a futile request. Probably nobody knew exactly how far Copernicus had progressed with his work until Georg Joachim Rheticus (1514–1576), a young scholar from Wittenberg, Germany, arrived in Frauenburg in 1539.

In 1540 Rheticus printed a summary of Copernicus's nearly completed book, *De revolutionibus orbium coelestium* (Revolutions of the heavenly spheres). The summary was known as the *Narratio prima* (First report). Two years later Rheticus was instrumental in having a portion of the book published in Nuremberg. When he took a position at the University of Leipzig, the publication process was taken over by Andreas Osiander (1498–1552), a Lutheran clergyman. Osiander worked with an editor at the printing press. Osiander might have been the one who gave the work its title, *De revolutionibus orbium coelestium,* which is not found in the manuscript. The editor did not use Copernicus's introduction, which stated his theory as actual proof of a Sun-centered universe. Instead, the editor inserted an unsigned preface written by Osiander, which presented the observations simply as a

# "I too began to consider."

Only hours before Nicolaus Copernicus died in 1543, he received a copy of *De revolutionibus orbium coelestium,* which had just been published at Nuremberg, Germany. In this revolutionary six-volume work, Copernicus proposed his theory of a Sun-centered universe. Copernicus had written an introduction stating the theory as actual proof, but it was not included in the book. Instead, the editor had inserted an unsigned preface, written by Lutheran minister Andreas Osiander, that presented the observations simply as a method for calculating the positions of heavenly bodies. The editor did include Copernicus's dedication of the book to Pope Paul III, in which the astronomer explained his reasons for making his discoveries public. Following is an excerpt from the dedication.

*For a long time then, I reflected on this confusion in the astronomical tradi-*

*tions concerning the derivation of the motions of the universe's spheres. I began to be annoyed that the movements of the world machine, created for our sake by the best and most systematic Artisan of all [God], were not understood with greater certainty by the philosophers, who otherwise examined so precisely the most insignificant trifles of this world. For this reason I undertook the task of rereading the works of all the philosophers which I could obtain to learn whether anyone had ever proposed other motions of the universe's spheres than those expounded by the teachers of astronomy in the schools. And in fact I found in Cicero that Hicetas supposed the earth to move. Later I also discovered in Plutarch that certain others were of this opinion.... Therefore, having obtained the opportunity from these sources, I too began to consider the mobility of the earth.*

*Nicholas Copernicus. "Letter to Pope Paul III." Preface to* De Revolutionibus, *as quoted in* Nicholas Copernicus on the Revolutions. *Translated and edited by Edward Rosen.*

method for calculating the positions of heavenly bodies. The editor did include Copernicus's dedication of the book to Pope Paul III (1468–1549; reigned 1534–49), which explained his reasons for making his discoveries public (see accompanying box). The printed copy of the final volume of the six-volume work reportedly reached Copernicus only a few hours before his death on May 24, 1543.

## Initiates scientific revolution

The thousand copies of the first edition of *De revolutionibus orbium coelestium* did not sell out, and the work was reprinted only three times prior to the twentieth century. Scientists point out that Copernicus could have done a better job as an observer. He added only twenty-seven observations, an exceedingly meager amount, to the data he took from Ptolemy and from more recent astronomical tables. The accuracy of predicting celestial phenomena on the basis of his system did not exceed the accuracy achieved by Ptolemy. Nevertheless, Copernicus gave important information about the orbits of the planets, and the strength of his work was its appeal to simplicity. For instance, the rotation of the Earth made unnecessary the daily revolution of thousands of stars. In addition, the orbital motion of the Earth fitted perfectly with its period of 365 days into the sequence set by the periods of other planets.

In the tenth chapter of the first book of *De revolutionibus orbium coelestium* Copernicus compared the Sun to a lamp that lights up the whole universe: "In the center rests the sun. For who would place this lamp of a very beautiful temple in another or better place than this wherefrom it can illuminate everything at the same time." Seventy years later his heliocentric theory of the universe was proven by Galileo. Copernicus is now considered the father of modern astronomy. His work was the first step in the scientific revolution developed by the German astronomer **Johannes Kepler** (1571–1630; see entry), Galileo, and other scientists in the seventeenth century.

## For More Information

### Books

Rosen, Edward, translator and editor. *Nicholas Copernicus on the Revolutions.* Baltimore, Md.: Johns Hopkins University Press, 1978.

Veglahn, Nancy. *Dance of the Planets: The Universe of Nicolaus Copernicus.* New York: Coward, McCann & Geohegan, 1979.

Westman, Robert S., ed. *The Copernican Achievement.* Berkeley: University of California Press, 1975.

### Web Site

"Copernicus, Nicolaus." *Britannica.com.* [Online] Available http://www.britannica.com/search?query=copernicus&ct=&fuzzy=N, April 5, 2002.

Knight, Kevin. "Nicholas Copernicus." *Catholic Encyclopedia.* [Online] Available http://www.newadvent.org/cathen/04352b.htm, November 8, 2001.

"Nicolaus Copernicus." *Conventional Wisdom: Selected Quotations Illustrating the Illusions of Popular History.* [Online] Available http://www.ari.net/cw/cw.html#copernicus, April 5, 2002.

# Albrecht Dürer

**May 21, 1471**
**Nuremberg, Germany**
**April 6, 1528**
**Nuremberg, Germany**

**Engraver, painter**

"My affairs will go as ordained in Heaven."

*Albrecht Dürer.*

**Albrecht Dürer.**
*Reproduced by permission of*
*AP/Wide World Photos.*

The German painter and graphic artist Albrecht Dürer introduced the achievements of the Italian Renaissance into northern European art. The Renaissance was a cultural revolution that began in Italy during the mid-1300s. It was initiated by scholars called humanists who promoted the human-centered values of ancient Greece and Rome. Humanist ideals were soon influencing the arts, literature, philosophy, science, religion, and politics in Italy. During the early fifteenth century, innovations of the Italian Renaissance began spreading into the rest of Europe and reached a peak in the sixteenth century. Dürer's influence was most widely felt through his woodcuts and engravings.

During the fifteenth century, the Rhineland (a region along the Rhine River in Germany) and southern Germany were the foremost centers for the early printing and publishing industry. The industry was based on the technology of printmaking, which involved reproducing text and images from woodcuts and engravings. After the invention of movable type in the mid-1400s (see **Johannes Gutenberg** entry), woodcuts were used for illustrating books that were

## Woodcuts and Engravings

During the fifteenth century, the Rhineland and southern Germany were the foremost centers for the early printing and publishing industry. Woodcuts could be created with a minimum of technological expertise. To make a woodcut, an image was drawn onto a flat plank of fairly hard wood, such as pearwood. The wood was cut away from the sides of the lines, leaving the image in relief (raised above the surface). Ink was then applied onto the woodcut, which was pressed onto a piece of paper.

An engraving is made by cutting lines into a metal plate (usually copper). The cutting tool, called a burin, creates grooves of varying width and depth, depending on the pressure applied to it. Ink is spread onto the plate, and the surface is then wiped clean. A dampened piece of paper is put on top of the plate. Next the paper is covered with a piece of felt or blanket, and the two are run through a roller press. In the 1490s Albrecht Dürer raised the woodcut and the engraving to the level of high art.

produced on the printing press. By 1500 illustrated books were issued in great numbers north of the Alps (a mountain range between France and Italy). In the 1490s Dürer singlehandedly raised the woodcut to the level of high art. A much more complex technology was needed to manufacture a flat, smooth metal plate than to prepare a plank of wood. For that reason the production of engravings was more expensive, so it was usually confined to a local area. Engraving seems to have begun in the upper region of the Rhine River valley, near Lake Constance. Again it was Dürer who brought the Renaissance to the north by using engravings to reproduce fine art.

## Embraces humanism

Dürer was born on May 21, 1471, in Nuremberg, Germany. His father, Albrecht the Elder, was a Hungarian goldsmith (one who makes items from gold) who went to Nuremberg in 1455, where he married Barbara Holper, daughter of a goldsmith. The young Dürer received training as an engraver in his father's Nuremberg workshop. He made his first self-portrait, a drawing in silverpoint (a drawing technique using a pencil of silver, usually on specially prepared paper or parchment), at the age of thirteen. In 1490, after serving a four-year apprenticeship with the painter and woodcut illustrator Michel Wohlgemuth (1434–1519), Dürer set out on a trip through the Rhineland and the Netherlands. He then worked as a woodcut designer in Basel, Switzerland. In 1493 Dürer painted a self-portrait in which he represented himself in a romantic image. Above his head he inscribed these words: "My affairs will go as ordained in Heaven." The following year he returned to Nuremberg and married Agnes Frey. He then journeyed to Venice, Padua, and Mantua, where he copied works by the leading contemporary Italian masters. It is apparent in his drawings that he soon learned how to perfect anatomy and harmony (balanced relationship arrangement features) in his figures. He returned to Nuremberg in 1494.

During his travels, Dürer encountered humanism, the intellectual and literary movement that initiated the Renaissance. The Italian scholar and poet **Petrarch** (1304–1374; see entry) is credited with starting humanism in Florence in the mid-1300s. Soon other scholars were spreading his ideas throughout Italy and eventually into the rest of Europe. Humanism was being promoted in the Netherlands and Germany by the Dutch scholar **Desiderius Erasmus** (1466–1536; see entry). Humanists studied the works of Greek and Roman writers from ancient times (called the classical period) for the purpose of imitating them. Like the ancient Greeks and Romans, humanists valued the earthly life, glorified human nature, and celebrated individual achievement. As an expression of their optimism, Renaissance scholars defined a new area of learning called the "humanities," which initially included language and literature, art, history, rhetoric (public speaking), and philosophy.

Above all, humanists believed in the human potential to become well versed (knowledgeable) in many areas. Embracing this ideal, Italian artists absorbed a broad range of subjects and came upon new ways to view the world. One important discovery was perspective (also called single-point perspective), the technique used by painters to represent three-dimensional objects on a flat canvas (a cloth used for paintings) from a fixed point of view. The Florentine sculptor and goldsmith Filippo Brunelleschi (1377–1446) invented perspective when he was working on architectural drawings. Perspective eventually led to the concept of proportion, that is, the harmonious and balanced relationship of details in a work of art. The great Italian painter and sculptor **Michelangelo** (1475–1564; see entry) was one of the first artists to use perspective and proportion in his works.

Dürer absorbed many of these influences. He became interested in such humanist concepts as reviving the ancient use of allegory (a story featuring characters that have symbolic significance). He gained an appreciation of art theory (application of general principles to artistic creation), to which he later devoted much of his time. He also met prominent humanists such as the German scholar Willibald Pirckheimer (1470–1530), who became his lifelong friend. Dürer's travels opened his eyes not only to the marvels of ancient art but also to the variety to be found in nature. For instance, while working in Basel he created woodcuts as illustrations for books. These works show that he was a many-faceted artist who represented various aspects of daily life. He also captured views of the Alps Mountains (a mountain range between France and Italy) in landscape drawings and watercolors.

## Takes art in new direction

Upon returning to Nuremberg, Dürer established a workshop and entered one of the most productive periods of his career. The year 1498 was a momentous one, both for Dürer and for the art world in northern Europe. Until the end of the fifteenth century, art in northern Europe and in Italy had developed more or less independently of each other. Italian artists were using perspective and proportion to represent figures and objects that seemed actually to exist in space. Painters from Germany and the Netherlands, on the other hand, were producing essentially flat images that did not portray spatial relationships. Another important distinction was that Italian artists were promoting idealized concepts of beauty with refined, carefully balanced images that gave a sense of harmony and unity. The works of artists from Germany and the Netherlands were less refined, relying on a more "realistic" style that gave figures and objects a rougher appearance. Dürer was, in effect, the first non-Italian artist to introduce humanist concepts into the creation of art.

In 1498 Dürer painted his famous second self-portrait, which marked a turning point in his art. He represented himself as a humanist scholar and an elegant young man, suggesting that the artist is a member of the cultural elite instead of being merely a craftsman. This was a new concept, widely accepted in Italy, that raised the artist to the status of a creative genius. The idea had not yet reached northern Europe. At that time northern artists were still considered craftsmen, and their work was viewed as simply decorative and functional. Dürer wanted to pass his ideas along to a younger generation of artists, but he found that talented young German artists were not taught the fundamentals of painting. He therefore decided to teach them geometry, which he believed was the basis of painting. (Geometry is the branch of mathematics that deals with the measurement, properties, and relationships of points, lines, angles, surfaces, and solids.)

In 1498 Dürer published the last of fifteen woodcuts in a series titled *Apocalypse.* Using experimental techniques that combined the realistic style of northern art with the Italian concept of ideal beauty (perfect balance and harmony among all elements, such as shapes and colors, in paintings), he explored greater expression of form, texture, and light in woodcuts. *Apocalypse* is based on the fantastic images described in the Book of Revelation (also known as Apocalypse), the last book of the New Testament in the Bible (the Christian holy book). Revelation was possibly written by Saint John (called the Apostle; first century A.D.) while in exile with other Christians on the Island of Patmos off the coast of Asia Minor. They had fled there in A.D. 81 after being persecuted by Roman Emperor Domitian (A.D. 51–96). Depicting an apocalypse (a great catastrophe that brings momentous change), Revelation contains visions of triumph over evil and persecution. The book is organized according to patterns of sevens. Among them is the opening of the seven seals on the scroll in the hand of God. Four of the scrolls reveal the Four Horsemen of the Apocalypse, who will bring the catastrophe. The rider on the white horse is generally thought to symbolize Christ, and the rider on the red horse is war. Famine (widespread hunger resulting from lack of food) rides the black horse, and death rides the pale horse.

The Four Horsemen were included in the images Dürer depicted in *Apocalypse.* The results were dramatic. Never before had the terror of the Four Horsemen seemed so real as in Dürer's woodcut. Likewise, the artist convincingly portrayed an angel dissolving into a band of clouds in *St. John Eating the Book,* another woodcut in the series. Now considered the highest achievement in German woodcut art, *Apocalypse* presented biblical teachings in a new and understandable language that shows strong humanist influences. Dürer later created a series of prints representing the Passion (crucifixion) of Christ (*Great Passion,* 1511; *Small Passion,*1511 and 1513; and *Life of the Virgin,* 1500–11). This work is also notable for its innovative, humanist style.

Dürer revealed humanist influences in other works. He used perspective in the *Paumgartner Altarpiece* (1504). His portraits, such as *Oswolt Krell* (1499), were characterized by sharp psychological insight. He depicted mythological and allegorical subjects in engravings on metal, such as the *Dream of the Doctor* (after 1497) and *Sea Monster* (c. 1498). Dürer also used that technique for one of his most popular prints, *Prodigal Son* (c. 1496). It is based on the New Testament story of a young man who leaves home and leads a wasteful life, then repents and returns home to a joyful welcome from his father. In the print Dürer represented the son in a novel way. He chose not to depict the young man's sinful life or to show the happy reunion between father and son. Instead, Dürer captured the moment when the son becomes aware of his sinful ways and begins his repentance. This was a significant approach because the focus was on the son's emotions, which was consistent with the emphasis on the individual. In *Nemesis* (1502) Dürer showed his knowledge of human anatomy. The print also reflects his interest in allegory.

## Supports Reformation

Dürer went to Venice again in 1505. The following year he painted *Feast of the Rose Garlands* for the Chapel of Saint Bartholomew, the German merchants' church in Venice. The artist's use of bright colors and the techniques of perspective and proportion show the influence of Renaissance painters. After returning to Nuremberg, Dürer painted several large altarpieces (works hung above altars in churches), which combined colorful Italian features with the traditional northern style. Among them are *Martyrdom of the Ten Thousand* (1508) and *Adoration of the Trinity* (1511), which

*Melencolia I,* one of the three Master Engravings by Albrecht Dürer. ©*Historical Picture Archive/Corbis. Reproduced by permission of Corbis Corporation.*

show little figures in vast landscapes. Dürer then left painting and returned to print-making. Perhaps his most important works of the period from 1513 to 1520 were his engravings, which show the influence of his friendships with distinguished German humanists. The three so-called Master Engravings—*Knight, Death, and the Devil* (1513), *St. Jerome in His Study* (1514), and *Melencolia I* (1514)—represent the height of Dürer's engraving style and also express his thoughts on life, man, and art. These engravings are allegories of the three kinds of virtue associated with the three realms of human activity—action, contemplation, and intellectual pursuit. The active realm is depicted in *Knight;* the contemplative, in *St. Jerome;* and the intellectual, in *Melencolia I.*

Dürer gave equal attention to the world around him. Throughout his life he drew and engraved simple motifs studied from life, as in the dramatic drawing of his aging mother, who is emaciated (extremely thin) and ill (1514). Until 1519 Dürer worked for Holy Roman Emperor Maximilian I (1459–1519). He was involved in various allegorical and decorative projects, most of them prints, such as *Triumphal Arch* and *Triumphal Procession of Maximilian I.* Dürer also did some miniatures, such as drawings in the *Maximilian I Prayer Book* (1515).

In 1520 Dürer left Nuremberg for Antwerp, Belgium, to collect his yearly salary from **Charles V** (1500–1558; see entry), the new Holy Roman Emperor. This trip was a triumph for the artist and proved that he was held in high esteem. In his travel journal, Dürer left a daily record of his stay in Antwerp and of his visits to various Dutch, Belgian, and German towns. He met princes, rich merchants, and great artists. He drew portraits, landscapes, and townscapes in his sketchbook. He met Erasmus, whom he admired and of whom he made a portrait drawing, which he later engraved.

## Lucas Cranach the Elder

Lucas Cranach the Elder (1472–1553) was a German painter, printmaker, and book illustrator who helped promote the Protestant Reformation. Born in Kronach, near Bamberg, he was trained by his father. Almost nothing is known of his early career, except that he absorbed the revolutionary style of Albrecht Dürer. Cranach went to Vienna, Austria, in 1502. There he entered a humanist circle centered on the university and led by the poet Conrad Celtis (1459–1508). In Vienna, Cranach made religious paintings with a new expressive power. By loosely applying colors, he gave a sense of turbulence to figures, and he set them in agitated landscapes that seems to reflect their emotions. These works, especially their rendering of nature, influenced other artists in the Danube River region, including Albrecht Altdorfer (c. 1480–1530).

By 1505 Cranach had moved to Wittenberg, Germany, where he became court painter of the Saxon elector (representative for the district of Saxony to the imperial court) Frederick the Wise. Serving three more electors over the next fifty years, Cranach dominated the art of northern and eastern Germany through his works for the princes. He also produced work for the Protestant cause, which was centered in Wittenberg. His shop employed his sons Hans (c. 1513–c. 1537) and Lucas, called the Younger (1515–1586), plus apprentices and assistants. Cranach was Renaissance Germany's most prolific portraitist. Along with likenesses of Saxon nobles, he portrayed Protestant reformers in paintings and prints that spread the Protestant cause well beyond Wittenberg.

Cranach's links to the Protestant reformer Martin Luther (1483–1546) were both personal and professional. The men were godfathers to one another's children, and they collaborated on projects, such as anti-Catholic pamphlets, diagrams of reform doctrines, and illustrations for Luther's Bible translations. Nevertheless, Cranach continued to work for Catholic patrons, notably Luther's foe, Albrecht of Brandenburg. After his death his shop continued to thrive under Lucas the Younger.

During the final decade of his life, Dürer supported the ideas of Protestant reformer **Martin Luther** (1483–1546; see entry). Dürer's last great work was a two-panel painting, often called *Four Apostles* (1526). The monumental, sculpture-like figures represent Saints John and Peter (left panel) and Saints Mark and Paul (right panel). The paintings were probably intended as the wings of a triptych (three-panel artwork), but Dürer did not paint the central panel. He gave *Four Apos-*

*tles* to the Town Council of Nuremberg. In the panels he included quotations from the writings of the saints, which contained accusations against "false prophets," or those who falsely claimed to speak the word of God. Dürer's work proclaimed the unity of the new Protestant faith against the different sects arising at that time. In 1525 Dürer published a book on perspective (*Instruction in Measurement*), and his treatise on fortifications appeared in 1527. He died in 1528, a few months before the publication of *The Four Books on Proportions,* his last and most important theoretical work.

## For More Information

### Books

Hutchison, Jane Campbell. *Albrecht Dürer: A Biography.* Princeton, N.J.: Princeton University Press, 1990.

Raboff, Ernest. *Albrecht Dürer.* New York: Harper & Row, 1988.

### Web Sites

"Dürer, Albrecht." *MSN Encarta.* [Online] Available http://encarta.msn.com/find/Concise.asp?ti=038AD000, April 5, 2002.

"Dürer, Albrecht." *Webmuseum.* [Online] Available http://metalab.unc.edu/wm/paint/auth/durer/, April 5, 2002.

# Elizabeth I

**September 7, 1533**
**Greenwich, England**
**March 24, 1603**
**England**

**Queen of England**

Elizabeth I was queen of England and Ireland for forty-five years. During her reign she preserved stability in a nation divided by political and religious dissension, and she maintained the authority of the monarchy (government headed by one ruler) against the growing pressures of Parliament (British law-making body). Educated as a humanist, she supported the Protestant religion in England. (Humanism was a movement devoted to reviving the culture of ancient Greece and Rome, which gave rise to the Renaissance. Protestantism is a Christian religion that resulted from efforts to reform the Roman Catholic Church.) Elizabeth was not an active patron of Renaissance artists, choosing to focus more on politics than on culture. She was careful with her money and did not spend it on promoting art, architecture, and literature. Nevertheless, Elizabeth's court and her personal tastes inspired many of the creative efforts that mark her culturally successful reign.

"Though God hath raised me high, yet this I count the glory of my crown, that I have reigned with your loves...."

*Elizabeth I.*

## Early life troubled by father's actions

Born at Greenwich, on September 7, 1533, Elizabeth I was the daughter of King **Henry VIII** (1491–1547; see entry)

**Elizabeth I.** *Reproduced by permission of The Bridgeman Art Library.*

and his second wife, Anne Boleyn (c. 1507–1536). Henry VIII is best known today for establishing the Anglican Church (Church of England) after the pope, the head of the Roman Catholic Church, refused to let him get a divorce. Immediately after becoming king, Henry married his first wife, Catherine of Aragon (1485–1536) a staunch Catholic from Spain, and for more than a decade they were happy together. They had a daughter, Mary Tudor (1516–1558; ruled as Mary I, 1553–58), but the king wanted a son because he did not believe Mary would be accepted as the next monarch. (According to the so-called Salic Law, only a male could be the legitimate heir to the throne.) In 1527 Henry began demanding a divorce from Catherine so he could marry Anne Boleyn, who was an attendant in the court of Queen Claude of France. Henry was having a secret affair with Boleyn, and he hoped she might bear him a son. Henry incorrectly believed it was a woman's fault if she did not give birth to a boy.

Since England was still a Catholic country, the pope's consent was required before Henry could get a divorce. Pope Clement VII (1478–1534; reigned 1523–34) refused to grant Henry' request. Finally, the king acted on advice from his chief minister, Thomas Cromwell (c. 1485–1540), and simply announced that the pope had no authority in England. Laws passed by the Reformation Parliament in 1533 and 1534 named the king Supreme Head of the Church and cut all ties with Catholicism. The Anglican Church thus became an independent national body, based on some of the teachings of German reformer **Martin Luther** (1483–1546; see entry), who initiated the Protestant Reformation in 1517. (The Protestant Reformation was a movement that began as an effort to make reforms within the Roman Catholic Church and resulted in the establishment of the Protestant faith, which is separate from Catholicism.) Previously, Henry had opposed Luther and was rewarded by the pope with the title "Defender of the Faith." Now he accepted a number of Lutheran doctrines, such as rejection of the pope as God's sole representative on Earth, making the Church of England a part of the Reformation.

Henry's desire for a male heir made Elizabeth's early life very precarious. In May 1536 her mother was beheaded. Then on July 1 Parliament declared that Elizabeth and Mary were illegitimate (born to a man and woman who are not legally married) and that the right to the throne should pass to Edward

(1537–1553; ruled as King Edward VI, 1547–53) Henry's son with his third wife, Jane Seymour (c. 1509–1537). Even though Elizabeth had been declared illegitimate, she was brought up in the royal household. She received an excellent education and was reputed to be unusually talented, notably in languages (she learned Latin, French, and Italian) and music.

Elizabeth had a difficult time after her half-brother took the throne as King Edward VI in 1547. When Henry VIII died in 1547 Edward was crowned King Edward VI. Early in his reign, Elizabeth became romantically involved with Thomas Seymour (c. 1598–1549), the lord high admiral (highest-ranking officer in the British navy). Seymour was Edward's uncle and was involved in a number of schemes to gain more power. He wanted to marry Elizabeth, and he was attempting to replace his brother Edward Seymour, as the young king's protector. Thomas was also trying to arrange for his own ward (a young person under the care of a guardian), Lady Jane Grey (1537–1554), to marry King Edward. In January 1549 Edward Seymour had Thomas arrested for challenging his authority as protector of the king. As a result of Thomas's activities Elizabeth herself came under suspicion, and she and her entire household (attendants and advisers) were subjected to intense questioning. Thomas Seymour was executed for treason (betrayal of one's country) later in 1547. During this period she experienced ill health but pursued her studies under her tutor, Roger Ascham (1515–1568). In 1553, following the death of Edward VI, Mary became Queen Mary I with the intention of leading the country back to Catholicism (see accompanying box). The young Elizabeth found herself involved in the complicated situations that accompanied these changes. Without her knowledge Thomas Wyatt (1503–1542), a Protestant, plotted to put her on the throne by overthrowing Mary. The rebellion failed, and though Elizabeth maintained her innocence, she was sent to the Tower of London (a prison for members of the royalty and nobility). After two months she was released against the wishes of Mary's advisers and placed in an old royal palace at Woodstock. Later she was allowed to take up residence once again at Hatfield, where she resumed her studies with Ascham. On November 17, 1558, Mary died and Elizabeth succeeded to the throne. Elizabeth's reign was to be looked back on as a golden age when England began to assert itself internationally through the mastery of sea power. At the time she came to the throne, however, the condition of the country was far from stable, both internationally and internally.

## Deals with Catholic opposition

At the age of twenty-five Elizabeth was a rather tall and well-poised woman. What she lacked in feminine warmth, she made up for in the worldly wisdom she had gained from a difficult and unhappy youth. It is significant that one of her first actions as queen was to appoint William Cecil (1520–1598; later Lord Burghley) as her chief secretary. Cecil was to remain her closest adviser. They both knew that England faced political obstacles in France and Spain, the two great European powers at the time. Elizabeth and Cecil also knew that the key to England's success lay in balancing France and Spain against each other. This would ensure that neither country could bring its full force to bear against England.

England had experienced both a sharp swing to Protestantism under Edward VI and a Catholic reaction under Mary. The question of the nature of the church in England needed to be settled immediately, and it was debated in Elizabeth's first Parliament in 1559. Members of Parliament knew that keeping Catholicism as the official religion was not politically possible, which had been proven during Mary's reign. In 1559 Parliament passed the Acts of Supremacy and Conformity, which declared the Church of England as the official faith. This settlement represented more of a victory for Puritans than the queen desired. (The Puritans were a group of strict Protestants). It indicated to Elizabeth that her control of Parliament was not complete.

Though the settlement achieved in 1559 remained essentially unchanged throughout Elizabeth's reign, the conflict over religion was not stilled. The Church of England, of which Elizabeth was the supreme governor, was attacked by both Catholics and Puritans. Estimates of Catholic strength in Elizabethan England are difficult to make, but it is clear that a number of Englishmen remained Catholics on the surface. There was constantly the danger of a Catholic trying to take the throne. Elizabeth's foremost rival was her second cousin, Mary

## "Bloody Mary"

Mary Tudor took the throne as Queen Mary I in 1553. Like her mother Catherine of Aragon, Mary was pro-Spanish and Catholic. Soon after being crowned, she married Philip of Spain (soon to be King Philip II), but Parliament prevented him from taking the English throne along with his wife. Mary had widespread popular support, and she immediately began undoing reforms initiated by her father, King Henry VIII, and her brother King Edward VI. In 1553 she recognized the jurisdiction of the pope (head of the Roman Catholic Church in England). Many people supported Mary's restoration of the Catholic faith, believing that Edward's reign had gone too far in abolishing cherished ceremonies and beliefs.

Today Mary is best known as "Bloody Mary" because of her persecution (repression with violence) of Protestants. During her brief five-year reign nearly three hundred people were burned at the stake. This method of punishment, which was introduced by the Inquisition (an official Catholic Church court charged with finding heretics, or people who violate or oppose the teachings of the church), supposedly drove evil spirits out of the sinners. Many who refused to reject Protestant beliefs continued to worship secretly or fled to countries on the European continent. Others became involved in a series of plots against Mary's government. Protestant leaders looked to the queen's half-sister, Elizabeth, as a possible Protestant replacement. Mary then had Elizabeth arrested and sent to the Tower of London and then to Woodstock. Five years later Mary, who was now near death, named Elizabeth to be her successor.

Stuart, Queen of Scots (1542–1587; ruled 1542–87), who was held in custody in England from 1568 until Elizabeth ordered her execution in 1587 (see accompanying box). During this entire time, Parliament repeatedly pressed Elizabeth for harsher legislation to control the Catholics. It is apparent that she successfully resisted these pressures. While legislation against Catholics did become progressively sterner, the queen was able to limit the severity of its enforcement and retained the loyalty of many English people who were sympathetic to Catholicism.

For their part the Puritans waged a long battle in the church, in Parliament, and in the country at large for stricter enforcement of the Acts of Supremacy and Conformity. Under the influence of leaders like Thomas Cartwright and John Field, and supported in Parliament by the brothers Paul and Peter Wentworth, the Puritans subjected the religious settlement to great stress. The queen found that she could control Parliament through her councilors and the force of her own personality. It was, however, some time before she could control the church and the country as effectively. It was only with the naming of John Whitgift (1530–1604) as the Archbishop of Canterbury (head administrator of the Church of England) that she found her most effective weapon against the Puritans. With the majority of royal support, Whitgift was able to use the machinery of church courts to curb the Puritans. By the 1590s the Puritan movement was in serious trouble. Many of its prominent patrons were dead, and with the publication of *Marprelate Tracts,* a bitter satire (criticism with humor) against the monarchy, some Puritan leaders brought the movement into great disfavor.

## Conducts effective foreign policy

When Elizabeth became queen, England was not strong enough militarily or economically to oppose either France or Spain. England was already at war with France, however, and Elizabeth quickly brought this conflict to a close. Throughout the early years of her reign, France appeared to be the chief foreign threat to England because of the French connections of Mary, Queen of Scots. The Scottish queen had lived at the French court and was educated in France. In 1560 Elizabeth signed the Treaty of Edinburgh, an alliance between England and Scotland, which eliminated the threat that France posed through Scotland. Wars between Catholics and Huguenots (French Protestants) in France also aided the English cause. Equally crucial was the fact that Philip II of Spain was not anxious to further the Catholic cause in England so long as its chief beneficiary would be Mary, Queen of Scots. If he assisted her, he would essentially be aiding his French rivals.

In the 1580s Spain emerged as the chief threat to England. During the years 1570 to 1585 there was neither war nor peace, but Elizabeth found herself under increasing pressure from Protestant activists to take a firmer line against Catholic Spain. She authorized voyages of privateers (private ships commissioned by a government to attack enemy ship-

## The Tale of Two Queens

In 1568 Mary, Queen of Scots, fled into England to escape religious and political revolt being stirred up in her home country. Elizabeth's second cousin, Mary was the granddaughter of King Henry VII's sister Margaret and King James IV of Scotland. Mary was the rightful heir to Elizabeth's throne, but she was also a Catholic. Her presence was a political threat, especially in light of the English Parliament's continued efforts to marry off Elizabeth. The question of Elizabeth's marriage was largely responsible for England's foreign policy for the first twenty years of her reign. After 1578 her status as the "Virgin Queen" was accepted and celebrated by the poets of her court. Throughout this time, however, the Scottish queen would remain in England and be a constant source of political trouble. Finally Elizabeth was convinced, after the discovery of a treasonous plot, that Mary was conspiring against her. Elizabeth had Mary, Queen of Scots, executed in 1587.

ping vessels) against Spanish shipping, which only served to increase tensions between the two countries. In 1585 Elizabeth decided to intervene on behalf of the Netherlands (Holland) in its revolt against Spain. She sent an expeditionary force to the Netherlands, an act that meant the temporary end of the queen's policy of balance and peace. The struggle against Spain culminated in the English defeat of the Spanish Armada (a fleet of heavily armored war ships) in 1588. The victory was due to a combination of luck, poor Spanish military decisions, and English skill. In some ways it marked the high point of Elizabeth's reign, and the period that followed has been called "the darker years."

## The queen confronts problems

In spite of the spectacular defeat of the Spanish Armada, which established English dominance of the seas, Elizabeth encountered problems in the last part of her reign. During the 1590s she struggled to keep her government from going bankrupt (becoming unable to pay bills because of lack of funds). Yet she also spent excessive amounts of money on the "Cult of Gloriana" ("Gloriana" was a nickname given her by admirers), staging grand pageants and spectacles to impress the English people. Her final years were dominated by controversy surrounding one of her favorite courtiers (members of the court), Robert Devereux (1566–1601), earl of Essex. Essex had numerous clashes with William Cecil and his son, Robert Cecil (1563–1612). When William Cecil died in 1598, Elizabeth snubbed Essex and awarded her highest council post to Robert Cecil. Then in 1599 she placed Essex in command of a military force and sent him to Ireland to subdue Tyrone's Rebellion. This was a movement, led by Hugh O'Neill (c. 1540–1616), earl of Tyrone, to gain Irish independence from England. But Essex botched the job miserably. Not only did he refuse to follow Elizabeth's orders but he also signed an unauthorized truce with the rebels.

When Essex returned to England, Elizabeth reluctantly withdrew her support from him. In 1601 he attempted to stage a coup (overthrow of government) that would oust Cecil's party and put his own party in power around the queen. Essex sought aid from the army in Ireland and from King James VI (1566–1625) of Scotland. The plot failed, however, and Essex was arrested. He was put on trial and sentenced to death. After Elizabeth reluctantly signed the death warrant (document that authorizes a death sentence), Essex was executed. Another domestic problem was Parliament's fight over the granting of monopolies (exclusive control or possession of a trade or business). Elizabeth was able to head off the conflict by promising that she herself would institute reforms. In her famous "Golden Speech," which she delivered to her last Parliament, she proved that even in old age she had the power to win her people to her side. She said:

> Though God hath raised me high, yet this I count the glory of my crown, that I have reigned with your loves.... It is my desire to live nor reign no longer than my life and reign shall be for your good. And though you have had, and may have, many princes more mighty and wise sitting in this seat, yet you never had, nor shall have, any that will be more careful and loving.

These words concealed the reality of the end of Elizabeth's reign. Severe tensions did exist. The finances of the monarchy, exhausted by war since the 1580s, were in a sorry state, and the economic plight of the country was not much better. Parliament was already testing its power to dispute is-

sues with the monarchy, though members did hold back, perhaps out of respect for the elderly queen. Religious tensions were hidden rather than removed. For all the greatness of her reign, it was a shaky inheritance that Elizabeth passed on to her successor, King **James I** (1566–1625; see entry)—the son of her former rival, Mary, Queen of Scots—when she died on March 24, 1603.

**The English defeat of the Spanish Armada in 1588 marked the high point of Elizabeth's reign.**
*Reproduced by permission of The Granger Collection.*

## Reign marked by achievements

The long reign of Elizabeth I was darkened by the executions of Mary, Queen of Scots and Essex. Yet Elizabeth is best remembered for her accomplishments, such as strengthening the Anglican Church and keeping government finances stable. Most of all, she embodied the spirit of her people—a determination to survive and indeed prosper in the face of enormous odds. Elizabeth's court became the cultural center of its day, and her era was a time of unparalleled literary achievement. Edmund Spenser (see box in **William Shake-speare** entry) dedicated his masterpiece, the epic poem *The Fairie Queen,* to Elizabeth. Dramas by the playwright William Shakespeare (1564–1616) and his contemporaries rank among the highest achievements of the Elizabethan age.

During Elizabeth's reign England also began emerging as a great sea power, which eventually gave rise to the expansion of the British Empire over the next three centuries. The most famous exploits were made by the navigators John Hawkins (1532–1595) and Francis Drake (c. 1543–1596). Hawkins opened up English trade with islands in the Caribbean Sea in the New World (the European term for the Americas), and Drake circumnavigated (sailed around) the globe between 1577 and 1580. There were efforts to colonize Virginia, the territory in North America named in Elizabeth's honor. English settlers made three failed attempts to start a colony at Roanoke, an island off the coast of Virginia. The last group of colonists mysteriously disappeared. The first successful English colony in North America was Jamestown, Virginia, which was started in 1607 during the reign of Elizabeth's successor, James I.

## For More Information

### Books

Brimacombe, Peter. *All the Queen's Men: The World of Elizabeth I.* New York: St. Martin's Press, 2000.

Plowden, Alison. *The Young Elizabeth: The First Twenty-Five years of Elizabeth I.* Stroud, Gloucestershire: Sutton, 1999.

Starkey, David. *Elizabeth: The Struggle for the Throne.* New York: HarperCollins, 2001.

Thomas, Jane Resh. *Behind the Mask: The Life of Queen Elizabeth I.* New York: Clarion Books, 1998.

### Web Sites

"Elizabeth I." *Tudor Royal History.* http://www.royalty.nu/Europe/England/ Tudor/ElizabethI.html, April 5, 2002.

Halsall, Paul. "Elizabeth I." *Modern History Sourcebook.* http://www.fordham.edu/halsall/mod/elizabeth1.html, April 5, 2002.

Jokinen, Anniina. "Elizabeth I." *Luminarium.* [Online] Available http://www.luminarium.org/renlit/eliza.htm, April 5, 2002.

# Desiderius Erasmus

**October 27, 1466**
**Rotterdam, Netherlands**
**July 12, 1536**
**Basel, Switzerland**

**Humanist scholar**

The Dutch scholar Desiderius Erasmus was the foremost humanist in northern Europe (see accompanying box for a description of humanism). He promoted a method called philology (study of language used in literary texts) in the study of the Bible (the Christian holy book). Erasmus also popularized works by ancient and early Christian writers. Known as a "Christian humanist," he combined Christian teachings with classical ideals. In his own time, even critics did not dispute that he was the reigning "prince of humanists." His admirers credited him with the single-handed revival of literary study in Germany. For some years Erasmus enjoyed celebrity status. He was sought after by other scholars who conducted extensive letter exchanges with him, and visitors considered a journey to his home a cultural pilgrimage (religious journey). Many of his works, such as *Handbook of the Christian Soldier* and *Praise of Folly,* were translated into all major European languages. Erasmus's reputation began to decline in the 1520s, however, when he refused to take sides in the debate surrounding the Protestant Reformation (a movement to reform the Roman Catholic Church). By the end of his life he was being charged with disloyalty by Protestants and Catholics alike.

"In the country of the blind the one-eyed man is king."

*Desiderius Erasmus.*

**Desiderius Erasmus.**
*Drawing by Hans Holbein.*
*©Bettmann/Corbis.*
*Reproduced by permission of Corbis Corporation.*

## Criticizes scholastics

Erasmus was born in Rotterdam, Holland, the illegitimate son of Roger Gerard, a priest, and a physician's daughter. Throughout his life he was sensitive about the lowly circumstances of his birth. He was orphaned at age five and placed under the care of guardians. From 1475 until 1484, Erasmus received a classical education from the Brethren of the Common Life. The Brethren was a religious community that reformed the educational system in the Low Countries (present-day Belgium, Luxembourg, the Netherlands, and parts of northern France) by replacing scholasticism with humanist concepts. Scholasticism had been the dominant method of study in the Middle Ages. Scholastics sought to combine Christian teachings with the concept of reason found in the works of ancient Greek philosophers. At the beginning of the Renaissance, a scholastic education consisted mainly of a series of exercises that subjected biblical texts to rational proof (logical reasoning). This development displeased many religious people, who felt such training failed to respond to the spiritual side of human experience. One result was the creation of the Brethren of the Common Life, which emphasized inner piety (dutifulness in religion). The Brethren schools provided a training ground for an impressive number of northern European humanists.

After completing his education, Erasmus entered the monastery (house for monks, members of a religious order) at Steyn in 1487. He was ordained a priest in 1492 and appointed secretary to the bishop of Cambrai (a city in present-day France) the following year. Erasmus's life took a significant turn in 1495, when he went to Paris, France, to study theology (religious philosophy). Paris was then the center of theological training in Europe. He lived at the Collège de Montaigu, a hostel (lodging house) for poor students. During his stay in Paris he developed a strong distaste for the scholastic method. In letters to friends Erasmus made scathing comments about the scholastic professors in Paris, whom he described as pseudotheologians (fake religious scholars) and obscurantists (those who make ideas unnecessarily complex).

Finding the living conditions at the Collège de Montaigu unbearable, Erasmus struck out on his own and began to tutor the sons of wealthy families. He never completed his degree in Paris. In 1499 he traveled to England with one of

## Agricola Introduces Humanistic Studies

"Humanism" is the modern term for the literary movement that initiated the Renaissance. Humanism was founded by the scholar and poet Petrarch (1304–1374) and his followers in Florence, Italy, in the mid-1300s. Humanist scholars believed that a body of learning called *studia humanitatis* (humanistic studies), which was based on the literary masterpieces of ancient Greece and Rome, could bring about a cultural rebirth (or renaissance). Humanistic studies consisted of five academic subjects: grammar (rules for the use of a language), rhetoric (art of effective speaking and writing), moral philosophy (study of human conduct and values), poetry, and history. The texts included not only classical literature but also the Bible (the Christian holy book) and the works of early Christian thinkers. The Dutch scholar Rudolf Agricola (Roelof Huisman; 1444–1485) is credited with introducing humanistic studies in northern Europe in the late 1470s and early 1480s.

Although Agricola's career was brief, he had a strong influence on hu-manism in northern Europe. Among his numerous works were orations, poems, letters, and Latin translations of Greek texts, most of which were published after his death. His greatest achievement was *De inventione dialectica libri tres* (Three books on dialectical invention), which was inspired by his discontent with current educational methods. Agricola's book was highly influential as a statement of humanist rhetoric, partly because he illustrated rules with detailed examples from classical works. Printed in 1515, *De inventione* was widely read by advanced students, professors, and theoreticians during the sixteenth century. One of Agricola's letters, *De formando studio* (On the organization of the program of studies), also influenced humanists. This letter became popular because it included a brief description of making a commonplace book, a collection of excerpts from ancient texts that provided models for teaching writing and recitation. The commonplace book was used in Latin grammar schools throughout Europe until the eighteenth century.

his pupils, William Blount, lord Montjoy. During his stay in England he made lifelong friends, such as the humanists **Thomas More** (1478–1535; see entry) and John Colet (c. 1466–1519). In 1506 Erasmus moved to Turin, Italy, where he obtained a doctorate in theology without meeting the requirement of being a resident student at the university. He then established a connection with the printing house of Aldo Manuzio (1449–1515) in Venice, which later contributed to his productive career as a writer.

## Writes *Praise of Folly*

By the time Erasmus returned to England in 1509, he was disillusioned with the Catholic Church. He disapproved of the wars that popes were always waging, and he was critical of clergymen who failed to fulfill Christian teachings in their own lives. As a result of this experience Erasmus wrote *Encomium moriae* (Praise of Folly), a satire (criticism through the use of humor) of the church and the clergy. In a famous passage a character named Dame Folly ridicules human folly (foolishness or lack of good sense) in general, but she focuses particularly on the self-importance of and lack of spiritual values among theologians and clergymen. The book concludes with an appeal to Christians to embrace what appears to be folly in the eyes of the world—that is, the simple-hearted devotion to the teachings of Christ, which leads to the Kingdom of Heaven. *Praise of Folly* made Erasmus famous. In 1515 he was appointed councilor to Prince Charles (later Holy Roman Emperor **Charles V**; see entry). To be near the royal court at Brussels in Belgium, Erasmus took up residence in Louvain, where he joined the theology faculty at the university. From the outset his relationship with other faculty members was an uneasy one because many of his writings drew criticism from theologians.

## Publishes New Testament

Erasmus was an unusually learned scholar and a highly prolific writer. He published innumerable works on a wide variety of subjects, including biblical studies, education, and religious reform. During his career he also wrote more than three thousand letters to kings, popes, scholars, financiers, humanists, and reformers.

Erasmus was best known for his edition of the New Testament, the second part of the Bible pertaining to the life and teachings of Jesus Christ (also called the gospels). Erasmus started his project in 1504, when he discovered a set of notes on the New Testament made by the Italian humanist Lorenzo Valla (1407–1457). Following in Valla's footsteps, Erasmus began making notes on differences and errors he found when he compared Latin translations with the Greek biblical texts. In his New Testament he presented the original version of the biblical texts, which was written in the Greek language, and placed it

**Desiderius Erasmus (seated) with his lifelong friends Thomas More, John Colet, and Ammonius at Oxford around 1500.** *Reproduced by permission of The Granger Collection.*

alongside a Latin translation. Released in 1516 Erasmus's book was the first published Greek text. It provided scholars and reformers with a basis for further study of the New Testament. Erasmus also published *Enhiridion militis Christiani* (Handbook of a Christian soldier; 1503), in which he described a tightly structured patriarchal (headed by men) society built on Christian values. Although he held traditional views on the role of women, he advocated education for women and emphasized mutual respect and fellowship in marriage.

Erasmus stated his educational views in *De pueris instituendis* (On the education of children; 1529) and other works, which were typical of humanist philosophy. He believed that parents had a duty to educate their children. If they could not give instruction themselves, they should select a teacher who could provide the necessary moral and intellectual guidance. Erasmus did not approve of physical punishment, and he recommended motivating learners with interesting material, a healthy challenge, and positive reinforcement.

His ideal curriculum (program of study) was based on language studies, the core subject of *studia humanitatis*. Another dimension to Erasmus's writing was *Querela pacis* (The Complaint of peace; 1517), in which he condemned war as an instrument of tyranny and warned rulers to fulfill their obligation to preserve Christian harmony.

## Drawn into Reformation debate

In the 1520s Erasmus was drawn into the Reformation debate. His position at Louvain became increasingly difficult because he was considered a supporter of **Martin Luther** (1483–1546; see entry), the German priest who initiated the Protestant Reformation in 1517. To escape the hostile climate, Erasmus moved to Basel, Switzerland, where he became the center of a scholarly circle that included many prominent humanists. He remained in Basel from late 1521 until 1529, when the city formally turned Protestant. At that point he went to Freiburg, a Catholic city in Germany. During the last decade of his life, however, controversy continued to swirl around him.

At the beginning of the Reformation, Erasmus had given Luther limited support, but he also voiced disapproval of Luther's radical language. When Erasmus saw that the changes proposed by Luther and other reformers would lead to a split in the church, he distanced himself from the movement. Although he preferred to stay on the sidelines, he finally had to defend himself against Catholic charges that he was a Lutheran supporter. In 1524 he wrote *De libero arbirio diatribe* (Diatribe on free will), in which he quoted biblical passages for and against the concept of free will (humans' ability to choose their own actions). He argued that in cases where Scripture is not clear on the matter, the church should be the final authority. Luther issued a sharp reply in *De servo arbitrio* (The bondage of the will), stating that humans do not have free will and insisting that this fact is clearly stated in Scripture.

## Condemned by the church

Many Catholic theologians thought Erasmus's contribution to the debate came too late, even though he had taken the side of the church. By this time he had already made theologians angry with *Praise of Folly,* in which he ridiculed the

A AMSTERDAM,
Chez DAVID MORTIER,

MDCCXIX.

church. But he had caused the most controversy with his edition of the New Testament. Although the book was welcomed by humanists, it was attacked by theologians. In the sixteenth century people believed that the Vulgate Bible (official Latin version) was written by Saint Jerome, in Latin, under divine inspiration (directly from the word of God). Since Erasmus had found errors in the Latin translation, he was charged with blasphemy (insulting God) and accused of giving support to

**An engraving of Desiderius Erasmus.** *Reproduced by permission of Mary Evans Picture Library.*

the reformers. From 1523 onward, Erasmus's works were investigated by the Paris theological faculty, whose judgment was considered the final word in religious matters. Numerous passages in his writings were censored (suppressed). In 1531 the church issued a formal condemnation and Erasmus gave a lengthy apology. Until his death in 1536 he was the focus of attacks from both Catholics and Protestants. Catholics continued to question his faithfulness to the church and Protestants called him a hypocrite (person who puts on a false appearance of virtue or religion) for his failure to support Luther.

The Reformation turmoil damaged Erasmus's reputation in Italy, France, and Spain. Elsewhere his books, especially his manuals of instruction and his editions of biblical texts, remained in use. The humanist tradition founded by Erasmus stayed alive in the Netherlands, and by the eighteenth century he was admired as the man who first presented a religion of reason. A resurgence of interest in Erasmus's writings also took place in the twentieth century, when world religions were seeking greater unity of thought. Historians suggest that the loss of life and devastation resulting from World War I (1914–18) and World War II (1939–45) made people more susceptible to Erasmus's pacifism (opposition to war). For instance, in 1950 a translation of *The Complaint of Peace* by José Chapiro was presented to the United Nations (an international organization founded for the preservation of world peace).

## For More Information

### Books

Hyma, Albert. *The Youth of Erasmus*. New York: Russell & Russell, 1968.

Vernon, Louise A. *The Man Who Laid the Egg*. Scottdale, Pa.: Herald Press, 1977.

### Web Sites

"Erasmus, Desiderius." *MSN Encarta*. [Online] Available http://encarta. msn.com/index/conciseindex/5A/05A6E000.htm?z=1&pg=2&br=1, April 5, 2002.

Koeller, David W. *Desiderius Erasmus*. [Online] Available http://campus. northpark.edu/history/WebChron/WestEurope/Erasmus.html, April 5, 2002.

Radice, Betty. "Erasumus." *Praise of Folly*. [Online] Available http://www. stupidity.com/erasmus/eracont.htm, April 5, 2002.

# Francis I

**September 12, 1494**
**Cognac, France**
**March 31, 1547**
**Rambouillet, France**

**King**

King Francis I of France was a true Renaissance monarch. The Renaissance was a cultural revolution that began in Italy in the mid-1300s. It was initiated by scholars called humanists who promoted the human-centered values of ancient Greece and Rome. Humanist ideals were soon influencing the arts, literature, philosophy, science, religion, and politics in Italy. During the early fifteenth century, innovations of the Italian Renaissance began spreading into the rest of Europe and reached a peak in the sixteenth century. Francis was devoted to making France a center of the Renaissance. He actively patronized (gave financial support to) painters, sculptors, architects, scholars, poets, and writers. Francis also practiced shrewd diplomacy (relations with other countries) and strengthened centralized rule in France. He was a man of immense charm and humanity who had a lust for life. He also was daring and courageous in battle. Yet there was a darker side to the gallant French king. Throughout his reign, Francis waged war against Spain for control of Italy, seeking revenge on his great rival, Holy Roman Emperor **Charles V** (1500–1558; see entry), who was also king of Spain. These wars were part of the conflict known as the Italian Wars (1494–1559), which began during

"I feed upon the good and put out the evil one."

*Francis I.*

**Francis I.** *Photograph courtesy of The Library of Congress.*

123

the reign of King Louis XII. Francis used deception in foreign policy, frequently breaking his solemn word in order to advance his own interests. Even though he was a Catholic, he formed alliances with Muslims (followers of the Islam religion) and Protestants (members of a religious group that broke away from the Catholic Church) to oppose Catholic Spain. Francis's final downfall was his futile rivalry with Charles V, which became his life-long obsessed.

## Achieves first military victory

Francis was born at Cognac on September 12, 1494, the son of Charles de Valois (died 1496), count of Angoulême, and Louise of Savoy (1476–1531). While his parents were fairly obscure nobles, Francis had a strong claim to the French throne. His father was a cousin of the king of France, Louis XII (1462–1515; ruled 1498–1515). Francis and his sister Margaret (**Margaret of Navarre**; see entry) were brought up in Cognac by their mother, who supervised their education. The young Francis learned the Spanish and Italian languages, and he spent his time admiring art and reading mythology, history, and literature. Surrounded by young playmates, he also learned the art of warfare and showed signs of unusual talent at the craft. When Francis was thirteen, he and Margaret left their mother's household to live at the French court, where courtiers (noblemen of the court) referred to Francis as the dauphin (elder son of the king). Louis XII granted him the duchy of Valois, created from the vast estates of the house of Orléans. In 1514 Francis married Louis's daughter, Claude de France (1499–1524).

Francis had his first experience as a military leader at an early age. In 1512 France went to war with Spain in the second phase of the Italian Wars (see accompanying box). Louis gave eighteen-year-old Francis command of an army. The Spanish king, Ferdinand II (1452–1516; ruled 1479–1516) of Aragon, had conquered and annexed the small kingdom of Navarre, situated between France and Spain on the Bay of Biscay. The French were now trying to recapture Navarre. Although Francis had able military advisers, he failed to score a victory. Then in 1513 Swiss troops inflicted a humiliating defeat on the French at Novara, a province in northwest Italy.

On December 31, 1514, Louis died, and on the first day of 1515 Francis took the throne as the king of France.

## Challenges Charles I

As king, Francis was primarily a man of action. He excelled in various outdoor sports and spent much of his time hunting. He and his court were constantly traveling. Whenever the king visited a town for the first time he was given an *entrée joyeuse* (joyful entry). Festivities included street theatricals and the erection of temporary monuments in his honor, adorned with inscriptions of praise and appropriate symbols of his royalty. Francis's personal emblem was the salamander and his motto was *"Nutrisco et extinguo."* Roughly translated, this means "I feed upon the good and put out the evil one." Popularly known as *le roi chevalier* (the knight king), Francis spent much of his reign fighting. He had an impressive beginning as a military leader. Determined to avenge the defeat at

**The meeting of Henry VIII and Francis I at the Field of the Cloth of Gold.**
*Reproduced by permission of Hulton Archive.*

**Field of the Cloth of Gold**

In 1520, Francis I met Henry VIII outside Guînes, France, at the Val Doré (Gold Valley). From June 7 until June 24, the kings and their courts engaged in "feats of arms" that were considered extravagant even by the standards of the Renaissance. Observers came up with the name "Field of Cloth of Gold" to describe the sight of so many luxuriously dressed nobles and servants. The occasion was the celebration of a treaty signed by France and England in March 1520. The agreement promised a new era of harmony among the major European powers: France, England, Spain, and the Holy Roman Empire. According to some accounts, however, Francis wanted to use the grand event to persuade Henry to join France in a war against Spain.

Henry and his entire court set sail for France, while thousands of French laborers completed work on magnificent tents, pavilions, and stands for the spectators. The French nobility set up elaborate tents of velvet and cloth made of gold. Francis's grand tent, also made of gold cloth, was supported by two masts (poles that support sails) from a ship tied together and surmounted by a life-size statue of Saint Michael (angel of the sword). Henry outdid Francis by building a temporary palace outside Guînes with a brick foundation, an edifice (house) of timber and can-

Novara by taking Spanish-held Naples, the young king personally led an army into Italy. In 1515, at Marignano (now Melegnano) near Milan, Francis won the greatest triumph in what was to be a long military career. His troops annihilated Swiss mercenaries (hired soldiers) under the command of Massimiliano Sforza (1493–1530), duke of Milan. In the aftermath of Marignano, Francis took the duchy of Milan, and Pope Leo X (1475–1521; reigned 1513–21) gave him neighboring Parma and Piacenza. The pope also entered into the famous Concordat of Bologna with Francis in 1516. According to the terms of the agreement, the Catholic Church in France came under direct control of the French crown.

Inspired by these victories, Francis openly challenged Charles I and **Henry VIII** (1491–1547; see entry), king of England, for election to the vacant throne of the Holy Roman Empire. The three young monarchs bitterly competed for the title of emperor, but the rivalry was especially intense between

vas made to look like brick, and large windows. On June 7 the kings and their courts of equal number, mounted on horseback, proceeded to the Val Doré and halted at opposite ends, as if arrayed for battle. Then, at the sound of a trumpet, Henry and Francis left their attendants behind. They galloped their horses toward each other, as if to engage in combat. Halting at a spot marked by a spear, the two kings embraced. After withdrawing to a nearby tent, they emerged two hours later and ordered their nobles to embrace one another.

The next stage was "feats of arms," which were meant to strengthen the embrace of reconciliation. They commenced on June 9 and consisted of jousting (combat with spears on horseback), open-field tournaments, and combat on foot. The only contest between the two kings appears to have been an impromptu wrestling match, in which Francis beat Henry. The celebration was solemnized in a mass on June 23. The next day, at the conclusion of the tournaments, the kings bade farewell and vowed to build at Val Doré a chapel dedicated to Our Lady of Friendship and a palace where they could meet each year. In 1521 England refused to acknowledge the treaty with France. In the aftermath the Field of the Cloth of Gold appeared as an act of frivolous diplomacy.

Francis and Charles. Charles's advisers bribed the German princes who served as electors, however, and in 1519 Charles took office as Holy Roman Emperor Charles V. As both the king of Spain and head of the Holy Roman Empire, Charles was now the most powerful ruler in Europe. In order to avenge this slight, Francis initiated the first of five wars with Spain and the Holy Roman Empire (Charles headed forces for both Spain and the empire). In 1520 Francis met with Henry VIII in Calais, France, at the Field of the Cloth of Gold (see accompanying box). Francis was hoping to win Henry's support in the war against Spain, but Henry declined to join the French effort. Meanwhile, Charles V had formed an alliance with Pope Clement VII (1342–1394; reigned 1378–94). In late 1520 Francis secretly backed a successful assault on the imperial city of Luxembourg (now in Belgium) and occupied Navarre.

During the next four years, however, the war in Spain went poorly for Francis. His men won a few battles, but they were finally driven out of Navarre. The Spanish then invaded France, taking Toulon and other parts of southeast France. Spanish forces also won victories against the French in northern Italy. In 1522 the French suffered a major defeat and lost the duchy of Milan. Complete disaster awaited Francis at Pavia, a city near Milan, in February 1525. He led an army of thirty-seven thousand men against a Spanish army of equal numbers. The Spanish lost one thousand men. Between ten thousand and fourteen thousand Frenchmen died, and many others were taken prisoner, including Francis himself.

## Violates treaty

Charles ordered that Francis be taken to Spain and placed under house arrest in Madrid. Although he was held for more than a year, the French king was not confined like most prisoners. He hunted regularly, enjoyed the companionship of his nobleman comrades, and attended numerous dinners given in his honor. He gained his release in 1526 by agreeing to sign the Treaty of Madrid, which required him to relinquish all claims to Italy and give up the duchies of Burgundy, Flanders (now part of Belgium, France, and the Netherlands), and Artois (a region in northern France). When Francis swore as a gentleman to return to captivity if he failed to live up to his end of the bargain, Charles agreed to set him free. Once he had returned to France, however, Francis declared the treaty to be null and void. His excuse was that he was forced to sign the document at a time when he could not think clearly.

Francis's violation of the treaty made another war with Spain inevitable. Francis quickly organized the League of Cognac (1526), which allied France, England, Milan, Venice, the Papal States (territories under the direct rule of the pope), and the republic of Florence against Charles. But in this second war, which began in 1527, Charles was destined to win an even greater victory. By 1529, Francis had signed the Treaty of Cambrai, which repeated the humiliating terms of the earlier Treaty of Madrid. It also called for Francis's two sons to be held in Madrid for a ransom (money paid for releasing a hostage) of two million gold crowns (a sum of Spanish money). In 1530 Francis married Eleanor of Portugal, a sister of Charles V.

## Seeks further revenge

For six years, Francis remained in France, where he devoted his time to the arts. By 1536, however, he was determined to seek revenge against Charles. Francis formed an alliance with the Ottoman leader Khayr ad-Din (pronounced kigh-ruh-DEEN; died 1546), who was called Barbarossa by Europeans. This move shocked and offended most Christians in Europe, even many of Francis's longtime supporters. Though they appreciated his will to resist the mighty Spanish kingdom, they felt that he was committing heresy (violation of church laws) by allying with "infidel," or non-Christian, Turks to slaughter fellow Christians. Charles launched a successful assault against Francis's Turkish ally in the Mediterranean Sea. Spanish forces led personally by Charles took La Goletta (now Halq al-Wadi), a seaport town in northeast Tunisia. Charles liberated thousands of Christian prisoners, and soon thereafter captured the port of Tunis. Barbarossa fled to Algiers (now Algeria), in North Africa, with the remnant of his fleet. Charles then turned toward Italy, landed in Sicily in August, and advanced with ease toward the Alps. He also invaded Provence, a region in southeast France, and areas of northern France. By 1538, when a peace agreement was signed at Nice, France, both sides were financially exhausted. In one year alone, Francis had spent 5.5 million livres (an amount of French money) on the war and had neither won nor regained any territory.

Francis mounted another war against Charles in 1542. This time he allied his forces with the Schmalkaldic League, a group of German Protestant noblemen who were opposed to Charles's policies. At Mühlberg, Germany, however, Charles won his greatest victory over Francis and the Lutheran princes. In 1545 Francis vented his anger on the Waldensians, a group of religious dissidents, in his own country. The Waldensians were advocates of the views of Peter Waldo (Pierre Valdés; died before 1218), an early French religious reformer who protested corruption in the Catholic Church. A brutal campaign against the Waldensians demolished twenty-two towns and killed four thousand people. Francis issued a list of banned books and established a court to punish heretics. The court burned hundreds of Huguenots (French Protestants) at the stake.

Francis died of gout (inflammation of the joints caused by imbalance in metabolism) and liver disease at Rambouillet, France, in 1547. At the time of his death, the French crown was six million livres in debt. Ten years later, France declared bankruptcy (lack of funds to pay bills). The Italian Wars finally ended after a seventh war, which lasted from 1547 until 1559. It was waged by the successors of Francis and Charles. In these wars, Spanish armies were victorious for the sixth time. As a result of the victory, Spain was given control of Italy in the Treaty of Cateau-Cambrésis in 1559.

## Leaves legacy in the arts

Although Francis failed in his military quest against Charles, he was remembered as a great patron of the arts who helped bring the Italian Renaissance to France. One of his pet projects was the renovation of the royal palaces at Blois, Chambord, Fontainebleau, and the Louvre. In 1515, after his conquest of Milan, Francis invited the great sixty-five-year-old Italian artist **Leonardo da Vinci** (1452–1519; see entry) to settle in France. The king gave Leonardo the manor of Cloux outside Amboise, where the painter spent the last three years of his life. He seems not to have painted anything for the king, but some of his notes and drawings date from his time in France. By 1545 several of Leonardo's major works, including the famous *Mona Lisa,* were part of Francis's collection. Francis also purchased the works of other Italian painters, including **Michelangelo,** (1475–1564; see entry) **Raphael,** (1483–1520; see entry) and Titian. For a brief time Francis employed the artist Andrea del Sarto (1486–1530). The king also collected drawings, sculpture, tapestries (large embroidered wall hangings), and precious objects.

Francis I has been called *"père des lettres"* ("father of letters"). He had several scholars in his court, including the French humanist Guillaume Budé (1467–1540), who wrote *L'institution du prince* (The institution of the prince). Francis also corresponded with the Dutch humanist **Desiderius Erasmus** (1466–1536; see entry) and sponsored a royal lecture series that supported promising scholars. The king liked books, and a chest containing his favorite books—mostly ancient histories and medieval romances—followed him on his travels.

He enlarged the library at Blois, which he had inherited. He employed agents in Italy and elsewhere to acquire precious classical manuscripts, many of them in Greek, for his library at Fontainebleau. The two royal libraries were integrated in 1544, eventually forming the nucleus of the present-day Bibliotèque Nationale in Paris. His paintings also were the beginning of the collection that is now in the Louvre, an art museum in Paris. In 1540 Francis ordered many of his books to be bound in tooled (decorated) leather. Printing was another of the king's interests. Three special fonts (style of writing used in printing) of Greek characters were cut by the French type designer Claude Garamond (c. 1480–1561) at Francis's expense.

Like many monarchs of the time, Francis was interested in the occult (supernatural) sciences—astrology (prediction of future events according to the positions of stars and planets), alchemy (science devoted to turning bases metals into gold), and the Kabbalah (Jewish mystical text). At the time these sciences were thought to hold the key to the secret forces of the universe. In 1530 the king created four royal professorships, two in Greek and two in Hebrew, to which others were added later. The Collège de France traces its origin to this foundation. In the sixteenth century Francis was commonly called "le grand roi François" ("the great king Francis"). Later he was known as a playboy (man who devotes his life chiefly to pleasure). Modern historians have reassessed this view, noting his impressive cultural legacy and his reign as a strong monarch.

## For More Information

### Books

Cox-Rearick, Janet. *The Collection of Francis I: Royal Treasures.* New York: Harry N. Abrams, Inc., 1996.

Knecht, R. J. *Renaissance Warrior and Patron: The Reign of Francis I.* New York: Cambridge University Press, 1994.

Seward, Desmond. *Prince of the Renaissance; the Golden Life of François I.* New York: Macmillan, 1973.

### Web Sites

"Francis I." *Encyclopedia.com.* [Online] Available http://encyclopedia.com /searchpool.asp?target=Francis+I&Submit.x=45&Submit.y=17, April 5, 2002.

"Francis I." *Infoplease.com.* [Online] Available http://www.infoplease. com/ce6/people/A0819430.html, April 5, 2002.

# Galileo Galilei

**February 15, 1564**
**Pisa, Italy**
**January 8, 1642**

**Mathematician, physicist, astronomer**

> "All truths are easy to understand once they are discovered; the point is to discover them."

*Galileo.*

**Galileo Galilei.**
©*Bettmann/Corbis.*
*Reproduced by permission of Corbis Corporation.*

The Italian mathematician, physicist, and astronomer Galileo Galilei (called Galileo) was the foremost scientist of the Renaissance. (The Renaissance was a cultural movement that began in Italy in the mid-1300s and was initiated by scholars called humanists who promoted the human-centered values of ancient Greece and Rome.) Now considered the "father of modern science," Galileo made revolutionary contributions to astronomy, physics, and scientific philosophy. In 1612 he shook the foundations of the scientific world by supporting the Sun-centered theory of the universe, which the Polish astronomer **Nicolaus Copernicus** (1473–1543; see entry) had formulated nearly seventy years earlier. This daring assertion brought Galileo into direct confrontation with the Roman Catholic Church.

The Sun-centered theory of the universe was controversial because it contradicted the seventeenth-century belief that the Sun and all the planets revolved around the Earth. Since the second century A.D., astronomers (scientists who study the stars and planets) had accepted the Earth-centered view, which was stated by the ancient Egyptian scholar Ptolemy (Claudius Ptolemaeus; c. A.D. 100–c. 170). Ptolemy followed earlier Greek thinkers such as Aristotle (384–322 B.C.), who concluded that the Earth is the center of a fixed and perfectly balanced heavenly system. Ptolemy's ideas were enforced by the church, which found supporting evidence in the Bible (the Christian holy book).

Copernicus gave proof of the Sun-centered universe in *De revolutionibus orbium coelestium* (On the revolutions of the heavenly orbs), which was published only hours before he died in 1543. At the time the book was not a source of controversy because the preface stated that the theory was not presented as fact. Although some church officials expressed concern about Copernicus's ideas, action was never taken against the book. The problem did return, however, after Galileo proved the Sun-centered theory. In 1616 church officials forbade Galileo to defend or teach *De revolutionibus orbium coelestium*. Although he agreed to follow church orders, he nevertheless continued to gather evidence that supported Copernican theory. In 1532 the church put Galileo on trial, unleashing a controversy that continued into the twentieth century.

## States theory of natural motion

Galileo was born in Pisa, Italy, the first child of Vincenzio Galilei, a merchant and musician who championed advanced musical theories of the day. The family moved to Florence in 1574, and that year Galileo started his formal education in the nearby monastery (house of a religious order for men) of Vallombrosa. Seven years later he entered the University of Pisa as a medical student. In 1583, while Galileo was at home on vacation, he began to study mathematics and the physical sciences. Galileo ended his medical studies and pursued the sciences, but financial difficulties forced him to leave the University of Pisa in 1585 before he completed his degree.

After returning to Florence, Galileo spent three years vainly searching for a suitable teaching position. During that time he wrote works that gained him a reputation as a mathematician and natural philosopher (physicist). He then secured a teaching post at the University of Pisa in 1589. From the beginning of his academic career, he was an eager participant in disputes and controversies. For instance, he made fun of the custom of wearing academic gowns. He was willing to condone ordinary clothes, he said, but the best thing was to go naked.

When Galileo's father died in 1591, Galileo was left to care for his mother, brothers, and sisters. As a result of this additional responsibility, he had to look for a better position. He found one in 1592 at the University of Padua in the Republic of Venice. In 1604 Galileo publicly declared that he supported Copernicus's theory of a Sun-centered universe. He then gave three public lectures before overflow audiences in Venice. He argued that a new star, which had appeared earlier that year, was major evidence in support Copernicus's views. More important was a letter in which he stated his theory of natural motion. By natural motion Galileo meant that a body will fall freely in space, and he proposed the law of free fall to account for this phenomenon. This concept contradicted the accepted view that the universe was a perfectly ordered and fixed system in which no body can freely move on its own.

## Comes into conflict with church

In 1609 Galileo learned about the success of some Dutch spectacle (eyeglass) makers in combining lenses (pieces of glass used for forming an image by focusing rays of light ) into what later came to be called the telescope (an instrument used for viewing distant objects such as stars and planets). He feverishly set to work, and on August 25 he presented to the Venetian Senate a telescope as his own invention. The success was tremendous. He obtained a lifelong contract at the University of Padua, but he also stirred up resentment when it was learned that he was not the original inventor. Within a few months, however, Galileo had gathered astonishing evidence about mountains on the Earth's Moon and about moons circling the planet Jupiter through the use of his telescope. He also identified a large number of stars, especially in the belt of the Milky Way (a galaxy, or very large group of stars, of which the Earth's solar system is a part). On March 12, 1610, all these sensational findings were printed in Venice under the title *Sidereus nuncius* (Starry messenger). The booklet took the world of science by storm. The view of the heavens drastically changed, and so did Galileo's life.

In 1610 Galileo accepted the position of mathematician in Florence, Italy, at the court of Duke Cosimo II de' Medici (1590–1621). He left behind in Padua his common-law wife (a woman to whom he was not legally married), Marina Gamba, and his young son, Vincenzio. He placed his two daughters, aged twelve and thirteen, in the convent (house of a women's religious order) of Saint Matteo in Arcetri. Galileo's move to Florence turned out to be highly unwise. In the beginning everything was pure bliss. He made a triumphal visit to Rome in 1611, and the next year his *Discourse on Bodies in Water* was published. In this work he disclosed his discovery of the phases of the planet Venus, which proved the truth of the Copernican theory that celestial bodies travel around the Sun. Two years later Galileo published his observations of sunspots (the dark spots that appear from time to time on the surface of the Sun), which embroiled him for many years in bitter disputes with the German astronomer Christoph Scheiner (1573–1650). A member of the Jesuit order (Society of Jesus) and based at the University of Ingolstadt, Scheiner had published observations of sunspots in 1612 under the pseudonym (pen name) Apelles.

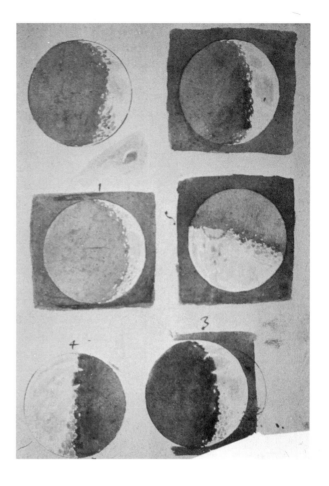

Sketches by Galileo of the Moon as he saw it through his telescope. *Reproduced by permission of The Granger Collection.*

## Church issues stern order

Galileo's aim was to make a detailed description of the universe according to the theories of Copernicus and to develop a new form of physics. A major obstacle was the traditional belief, stated in the Bible, that the Earth is the center of the universe. To deal with the difficulties raised by the Scripture, Galileo addressed theological (religious) issues. He was assisted by church leaders, such as Monsignor Piero Dini and Father Benedetto Castelli, his best scientific pupil. In letters to Dini and Castelli, Galileo produced essays that now rank among the best writings of biblical analysis of those times. His longest letter was addressed to Grand Duchess Christina of Tuscany. In all of the letters he discarded the idea of an Earth-centered universe in favor of the theory that the Earth revolves around the Sun. As the letters were more widely circulated, a confrontation with church authorities became inevitable. In 1616 Cardinal Robert Bellarmine issued an order that forbade Galileo to continue teaching or writing about the Copernican doctrine of the motion of the Earth.

Galileo agreed not to promote Copernicus's views. Nevertheless, he was determined to have the order overturned. In 1623 Galileo dedicated *Assayer,* a work on the philosophy of science, to the new pope (supreme head of the Roman Catholic Church), Urban VIII (1568–1644; reigned 1623–44). The next year Galileo had six audiences (formal meetings) with the pope. Urban promised a pension for Galileo's son, Vincenzio, but he did not grant Galileo permission to resume his work on a new description of the universe. Before departing for Florence, Galileo was informed that the pope had remarked that he did not believe the Roman Catholic Church would ever declare the Copernican theory to be heretical, but he was also certain the theory could never be proven. This news gave Galileo encouragement to go ahead with the great undertaking of his life, the *Dialogue Concerning the Two Chief World Systems* (known as *Dialogue*).

## Called before the Inquisition

Galileo's *Dialogue* was published in 1632. The book features four main topics discussed by three speakers on four consecutive days. The speakers are Simplicius, Salviati, and Sagredo, Simplicius represents Aristotle, Salviati is a spokesman for Galileo, and Sagredo plays the role of an arbiter (one who makes the final judgment on an issue), who leans heavily toward Galileo. The First Day is devoted to the criticism of the alleged perfection of the universe, as claimed by Aristotle. Here Galileo made use of his discovery of the "imperfections" of the Moon, namely, its rugged surface as revealed by the telescope. (Aristotle contended that the Moon's

## Starry Messenger

In 1610 Galileo published *Starry Messenger*, a booklet in which he recorded the results of observations with his newly invented telescope. He had gathered evidence about mountains on the Earth's Moon and about moons circling the planet Jupiter. He also identified a large number of stars. At the conclusion of *Starry Messenger* he summarized the evidence that supported the Copernican theory of a universe with the Sun, not the Earth, at its center. With a bemused tone he noted that some people were quite happy to accept the idea that planets revolve around the Sun. Yet they seemed to be offended by any notion that the Earth might move around the Sun along with the planets.

Galileo wrote:

*Here we have a fine and elegant argument for quieting the doubts of those who, while accepting with tranquil mind the revolutions of the planets about the sun in the Copernican system, are mightily disturbed to have the moon alone revolve about the earth and accompany it in an annual rotation about the sun. Some have believed that this structure of the universe should be rejected as impossible. But now we have not just one planet rotating about another while both run through a great orbit around the sun; our own eyes show us four stars which wander around Jupiter as does the moon around the earth, while all together trace out a grand revolution about the sun in the space of twelve years.*

The Achievement of Galileo. *James Brophy and Henry Paolucci, editors. New York: Twayne Publishers, 1962, p. 30.*

surface is perfectly smooth.) The Second Day is a discussion of the rotation of the Earth on its axis (an imaginary line extending through the center of the Earth from north to south) as an explanation of various celestial phenomena.

During the Third Day the orbital motion of the Earth around the Sun is debated. A main issue is the undisturbed nature of the surface of the Earth in spite of its double motion—that is, its revolving on an axis while at the same time orbiting around the Sun. The discussion on the Fourth Day shows that the tides (the rhythmical rising and falling of oceans and other bodies of water) are proof of the Earth's twofold motion. In this section Galileo seemed to contradict the contention of the Third Day discussion, that the surface of the Earth remains undisturbed by its double motion. The tides, which cause the regular movement of oceans, show that the Earth's surface is in fact affected by the twofold motion.

Church officials were outraged by the *Dialogue*, which proved that Galileo supported Copernicus's ideas. Galileo was summoned to Rome to appear before the Inquisition, a church court set up to punish heretics (people who violate or oppose the teachings of the church). The proceedings dragged on from the fall of 1632 to the summer of 1633. During that time Galileo was allowed to stay at the home of the Florentine ambassador in Rome. He was never subjected to physical force. Nevertheless, he had to inflict torture upon himself by publicly rejecting the doctrine that the Earth moved around the Sun. At the end of the trial, church officials ordered that *Dialogue* be placed on the Index of Prohibited Books by the Holy Office. The Holy Office was a branch of the church established as part of the Inquisition to review the content of all publications. The Index of Prohibited Books was a list of works that the church considered to be heretical.

## Remains a Christian

Galileo was confined to house arrest (he was not permitted to leave the premises) in Siena, a province in western Italy. He then received permission in December to live in his own villa at Arcetri. He was not supposed to have any visitors, but this order was not obeyed. The church was also unable to prevent the printing of Galileo's works outside Italy. Over the next five years translations of his writings were published in France and Holland. In 1638 his *Two New Sciences* was printed in Leiden, Holland. Like the *Dialogue*, this work is in the form of discussions over a period of four days. Topics included the mechanical resistance of materials, the atomic composition of matter, the nature of vacuum, the vibrations of pendulums, uniform and accelerated motion, and the projectile motion of a cannonball.

Although Galileo proposed a radically new concept of the universe, he remained a Christian to the end of his life. He believed that the world was made by a rational creator (God) who gave order to everything according to weight, measure, and number. Galileo stated this faith in the closing pages of the First Day of the *Dialogue*. He described the human mind as the most excellent product of the creator, because it could recognize mathematical truths. Galileo spent his last years partially blind, and he died in 1642.

## Would It Be "imprudent or unreasonable"?

In 1835 the Holy Office of the Roman Catholic Church removed Galileo's *Dialogue* from the Index of Prohibited Books. Yet more than one hundred fifty years would pass before the church officially made amends for the treatment Galileo himself had received at the trial in 1633.

On November 10, 1979, Pope John Paul II (1920– ; elected 1978) acknowledged that the church had caused Galileo to suffer a great. The pope called for a frank reexamination of the famous trial. On July 3, 1981, he appointed a special commission to study and publish all available documents relating to the trial. The pope presented the results of the commission's work to the Pontifical (Pope's) Academy of Sciences on October 31, 1992. The report made clear that astronomy was in a state of transition when Galileo was silenced in 1616 and when he was forced to withdraw his theory in 1633. Furthermore, scripture scholars were confused about cosmology (the study of the universe). The report stated that Galileo had not demonstrated the Earth's motion, and theologians had erred in their assessment of his teachings. But in the 1990s, the pope continued, science is so complex it is almost impossible to certify scientific discoveries as being absolutely true. The best one can hope for, he said, is that discoveries be "seriously and solidly grounded." He went on to state that the function of the Pontifical Academy was to advise the church if the degree of probability of a discovery is such "that it would be imprudent [unwise] or unreasonable to reject it." In other words, a scientific discovery should not be rejected if there is any possibility that it can be proven. Historians note that if such advice had been available to Pope Urban VIII, Galileo might have been spared the unhappiness of his final years.

## The aftermath

In 1820 the condemnation of Copernicanism was revoked (withdrawn) by the Holy Office. This action was taken on the basis of discoveries made by two little-known Italian astronomers. The first, Giovanni Battista Guglielmini, offered proof of the Earth's rotation by conducting experiments with bodies falling from a high tower. In Bologna, between 1789 and 1792, he made measurements and observed that the bodies deflected slightly to the east, thus proving that the Earth moves in a twofold motion. The second astronomer, Giuseppe Calendrelli, measured the parallax (the angular distance in direction of a celestial body, as measured from two points on Earth's orbit) of star Alpha in the constellation Lyra, also confirming such motion. He presented his findings to Pope Pius VII (1742–1823; reigned 1800–23) in a work published in 1806. During a debate over whether to approve an astronomy text in 1820, Benedetto Olivieri, head of the Holy Office, determined that the experiments of Guglielmini and Calendrelli demonstrated the Earth's twofold movement. Galileo's *Dialogue* was finally removed from the Index of Prohibited Books in 1835. But it was nearly one hundred sixty more years before the Catholic Church issued an official report stating that theologians had been wrong in their assessment of Galileo's teachings (see accompanying box).

## For More Information

### Books

Fisher, Leonard Everett. *Galileo*. New York: Macmillan, 1992.

Goldsmith, Mike. *Galileo Galilei*. Austin, Tex.: Raintree Steck-Vaughn, 2001.

Milton, Jacqueline. *Galileo: Scientist and Stargazer*. New York: Oxford University Press, 2000.

### Sound Recordings

Sis, Peter. *Starry messenger*. Prince Frederick, Md.: Recorded Books, 1997.

### Video Recordings

*Galileo: On the Shoulders of Giants*. Devine Entertainment, 1997.

### Web Sites

*Astronomy and Physics: Galileo*. [Online] Available http://webug.physics. uiuc.edu/courses/phys150/fall97/slides/lect06/, April 5, 2002.

"Galileo." *Encarta*. [Online] Available http://encarta.msn.com/find/Concise. asp?z=1&pg=2&ti=017E5000, April 5, 2002.

"Galileo." *The Quotations Page*. [Online] Available http://www.quotations page.com/quotes.php3?author=Galileo+Galilei, April 5, 2002.

# Artemisia Gentileschi

July 8, 1593
Rome, Italy
1652
Naples, Italy

Painter

T he Italian artist Artemisia Gentileschi (pronounced jahn-tee-LES-kee) is regarded as one of the important women painters of the Renaissance. (The Renaissance was a cultural movement that began in Italy in the mid-1300s and was initiated by scholars called humanists who promoted the human-centered values of ancient Greece and Rome.) She achieved international stature for her progressive style, ambitious range of themes, and strong feminist expression. Influenced by the innovative Italian painter Caravaggio (see box below), she adopted a dramatic, realistic style and a chiaroscuro technique (use of stark contrasts between light and dark). According to some accounts, Gentileschi was Caravaggio's student. Nevertheless, she departed from Caravaggio's, as well as other painters, models to develop her own themes. Her works feature biblical and historical women, whom she humanized and raised to heroic status. Gentileschi remained relatively unknown and unappreciated after her death. Then, in the twentieth century, art historians began identifying and collecting her work. Along with this belated recognition came a reassessment of her place in the history of European painting. Scholars note her role in transforming the

"The works will speak for themselves."

*Artemisia Gentileschi as quoted in* Artemisia Gentileschi and The Age of Baroque. *[Online] Available http://rubens.anu. edu.au/student.projects/artemi sia/Artemisia.html, April 5, 2002.*

**Artemisia Gentileschi.**
*Reproduced by permission of The Granger Collection.*

141

influence of Caravaggio in the use of chiaroscuro. Neverthe-less, the pictures show some distinctive traits of Gentileschi's own style, such as the depiction of authentic emotions. Examples are the alert stare of Judith as she beheads Holofernes and the startled expression of Susanna as she turns away from the elders.

## Works in Rome and Naples

In 1616 Gentileschi entered the Accademia del Disegno, becoming the first female member of the prestigious Florentine academy. She befriended the Italian astronomer **Galileo Galilei** (1564–1642; see entry), who was the court mathematician to Duke Cosimo II. Gentileschi returned to Rome around 1620. By 1624 she was presumably separated from her husband and was head of a household that included her daughter and two servants. Lacking access to large church commissions, Gentileschi found important private patrons. Her paintings *Cleopatra* and *Lucretia* (c. 1621) were purchased or commissioned by the Genoese nobleman Pietro Gentile. The Roman collector Vincenzo Giustiani owned her *David* (now lost), and in 1622 she painted her only surviving portrait for a sitter named Gonfalionere. After returning to Rome, Gentileschi abandoned the refined style that characterized her work in Florence and began to adopt a realistic technique that utilized chiaroscuro. Among her masterpieces from this period are *The Penitent Magdalen* (c. 1617–20) and another version of *Judith and Her Maidservant with the Head of Holofernes* (1625). This is a large, grand painting with a theatrical lighting effect that isolates the dramatic moment when Judith and her maidservants murder Holofernes. It may be connected with the popularity of the Judith theme in Roman theater at the time. Another majestic painting is *Esther and Abasuersus*.

Around 1628 Gentileschi moved to Naples. It was here that she began hiring assistants to paint architectural and landscape backgrounds in her works. In 1630 Gentileschi painted a self-portrait for the Roman collector-scholar Cassiano dal Pozzo. It was probably identical to her *Self-Portrait as the Allegory of Painting* (1630s). This picture is rendered in a strong chiaroscuro style, depicting Gentileschi in the act of

# Caravaggio

The Italian painter Caravaggio (Michelangelo Merisi; 1573–1610) was among the most innovative artists of the Renaissance. He often portrayed figures as if they were emerging out of darkness, with part of their faces and bodies illuminated by a bright light. Caravaggio revolted against both mannerism and classicism, the dominant artistic styles of the time. For instance, he rejected the elongated figures and curvilinear shapes of the mannerists. He also ridiculed the concept of the classicists that the subject of a painting should be idealized and carry a moral message. In *Bacchus with a Wine Glass* (c. 1595) Caravaggio showed not a Roman god but instead a pudgy, half-naked boy draped in a bedsheet, who is identified as Bacchus only by the vine leaves in his hair. Sometimes the subject was a scene from everyday life. For example, *The Fortune Teller* (c. 1595) shows an elegant young dandy with a sword at his side having his palm read by a Gypsy girl. He looks away with almost haughty boredom as she slips a ring off his finger. Caravaggio also liked to isolate a single instant in time. An example is *Boy Bitten by a Lizard* (c. 1593), which portrays a young man with a small girlish mouth and a rose behind one ear. He squeals with fright as a lizard comes out from behind a flower and bites him on the finger. One of Caravaggio's most famous religious works is *Crucifixion of St. Peter.* The saint is depicted at the moment when the executioners are beginning to raise up the cross to which he has been nailed upside down. His bare feet are thrust toward the viewer and the aged but powerful apostle lifts his head up from the cross in defiance.

Though Caravaggio was never truly famous in his own lifetime, many who knew his work realized they were seeing something amazingly new in his paintings. His style spread rapidly throughout Europe and influenced Artemisia Gentileschi, among others. Historians note that without Caravaggio, it is not possible to understand the works of the countless artists who followed in the seventeenth century.

painting against a dark background with light flooding onto her face and arms. The self-portrait is now famous as a celebration of the female artist. Other patrons in the 1630s included Francesco I d'Este (1610–1658), duke of Modena; Cardinals Francesco (1597–1679) and Antonio Barberini (1607–1671); and Ferdinando II de' Medici (1610–1670). From 1638 until 1641 she worked in England with her aging father at the court of King Charles I (1600–1649; ruled 1625–49) and Queen Henrietta (1600–1669). The Gentileschis decorated the ceiling of the Great Hall of the Queen's House

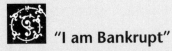

## "I am Bankrupt"

Gentileschi wrote many letters, some of which have been published. Of particular interest is a letter she sent in 1637 from Naples to one of her patrons, Don Antonio Ruffo, in Messina. Written on the day of her daughter's wedding, it provides a glimpse into Gentileschi's life as a successful but struggling artist. She indicates that her daughter was also a painter.

*My Most Illustrious Sir,*

*I wish to inform you that I received your letter of 21st February, so full of that kindness which Your Most Illustrious Lordship habitually conveys to your servant Artemisia, and with the enclosed note of exchange for one hundred ducats [an amount of Italian money]. I acknowledge also your commission for a work that I am to do for you. I hope with God's help to make something greatly to your liking, and Your Most Illustrious Lordship will see how much I value kindness in a noble heart.*

*I am very sorry that the Galatea [one of her paintings] was damaged at sea. This would not have happened if I had been permitted to carry out your orders myself, as I would have taken care of it with my own hands. But this will not happen again with the other work, as I will take it upon myself to follow your instructions.*

*As soon as possible I will send my portrait, along with some small works done by my daughter, whom I have married off today to a knight of the Order of St. James. This marriage has broken me. For that reason, if there should be any opportunity for work in your city, I ask Your Most Illustrious Lordship to assist me with your usual benevolence and to keep me informed, because I need work very badly and I assure Your Most Illustrious Lordship that I am Bankrupt.*

*Furthermore, I want Your Most Illustrious Lordship to promise me that as long as I live you will protect me as if I were a lowly slave born into your household. I have never seen Your Most Illustrious Lordship, but my love and my desire to serve you are beyond imagination. I shall not bore you any longer with this womanly chatter. The works will speak for themselves. And with this I end with a most humble bow.*

*Naples, today the 13th of March, 1649.*

*The most humble servant of your Most Illustrious Lordship,*

*Artemisia Gentileschi*

*Please send any letters you write to me in the name of Signor Tommaso Guaragna.*

Artemisia's Letter. [Online] Available http://rubens.anu.edu.au/student.projects/artemisia/Artemisia.html April 5, 2002.

at Greenwich. Gentileschi spent her final years in Naples. In the 1640s Gentileschi painted *Bathsheba*, a second *Susanna*, and *Lot and His Daughters*.

Artemisia Gentileschi wrote many letters that also reveal her determination to excel in the male-dominated art world. Her success in achieving that goal is seen in her influence on other European artists working in the late Renaissance. Among them were the Simon Vouet (1590–1649) in France, Giovanni Barbieri (called Il Guercino; 1591–1666) in Italy, Rembrandt (Rembrandt Harmensz; 1606–1669) in Holland, and possibly Diego Velázquez (1465–1524) in Spain. Many of Gentileschi's works were attributed to her father until the twentieth century, when art historians were able to identify her paintings.

## For More Information

### Books

Garrard, Mary D. *Artemisia Gentileschi Around 1622: The Shaping and Reshaping of an Artistic Identity.* Berkeley: University of California Press, 2001.

Lapierre, Alexandra. *Artemisia: A Novel.* Translated by Liz Heron. New York: Grove Press, 2000.

Vreeland, Susan. *The Passion of Artemesia.* New York: Viking, 2002.

### Video Recordings

*Artemisia.* Miramax Home Entertainment, 2001.

### Web Sites

*Artemisia Gentileschi and The Age of Baroque.* [Online] Available http://rubens.anu.edu.au/student.projects/artemisia/Artemisia.html, April 5, 2002.

"Gentileschi, Artemisia." *Web Galleries.* [Online] Available http://www.webgalleries.com/pm/colors/gentile.html, April 5, 2002.

Pioch, Nicolas. "Michelangelo Merisi da Caravaggio." *Webmuseum.* [Online] Available http://sunsite.unc.edu/wm/paint/auth/caravaggio, April 5, 2002.

# Johannes Gutenberg

**1398
Mainz, Germany
February 3, 1468
Mainz, Germany**

**Inventor, printer**

Johannes Gutenberg.
*Photograph courtesy of The Library of Congress.*

In the 1450s the German inventor Johannes Gutenberg perfected the printing press, which is recognized as one of the most important advances in Western (non-Asian) history. A mechanism by which small metal pieces engraved with single characters (letters) could be arranged to form words and sentences, the first press was used in Germany to print the Bible (the Christian holy book). Soon presses began to spring up all over Europe, and the impact was enormous. Literacy grew rapidly and knowledge spread as literature became readily—and affordably—available to many people for the first time. With the aid of printing, the ideas born in the Italian Renaissance (a revival of ancient Greek and Roman culture) during the late 1300s spread northward to France, England, Spain, the Netherlands, Scandinavia (Denmark, Sweden, and Norway), and eastern Europe during the fifteenth and sixteenth centuries.

## Printers use new technology

Around 1440 experiments with "writing mechanically" were being undertaken in three different areas of Europe.

Laurens Coster (c. 1370–c. 1440) of Haarlem, Holland, was said to be experimenting with a printing press. Although some historians have accepted Coster as the inventor of printing, most now give the credit to Gutenberg. The printing press combined two known but separate technologies, the screw press and the steel punch. The screw press consisted of a large upright screw that held two parallel frames. The screw press had long been used in linen, paper, and wine making. Printers adapted the frames of the screw press to hold "forms," or individual letters of the alphabet made of molded metal. The steel punch had been used by mints (places where coins are made) and goldsmiths to impress images on a softer metal and thus create a mold. Printers used this method to make molds for individual letters, whose "forms" were then cast in an alloy of lead, tin, and antimony (metallic element).

Fifteenth-century illustrations show three men—a compositor, an inker, and an operator—running a printing press. The compositor set letters in the two frames. The inker set the frames one above the other in the press, smeared them with ink, and inserted sheets of paper between them. The operator swung a lever to bring the two frames together and imprint two, four, or eight pages of text on each side of the sheet. The size of the book itself depended on the number of times a full sheet of paper was folded. The large folio (one fold, two pages) was used for academic works, and the smaller quarto (two folds, four pages) was used for literary texts. The still smaller octavo (four folds, eight pages) was at first used for Psalters and books of hours. Ideally, such a team could run off more than one thousand sheets from a pair of frames in a day's work, thus completing one part of the edition while the compositors prepared the frames for the next. But that meant working in close coordination. It took time to train a press team, and the printer had to buy the required equipment—press, types, and paper—before he could count on getting any money back from sales of a completed book. The risks involved in the printing business ultimately contributed to the failure of Gutenberg's own print shop.

## Suffers financial setbacks

There is no record of Gutenberg's whereabouts after 1444, but he appears again in Mainz according to a document dated October 1448. By 1450 he is known to have had a printing plant. He borrowed eight hundred guilders (a type of money) from the rich financier Johann Fust (1400–1466) for tools and equipment. In December 1452 Gutenberg had to pay off his debt. When he was unable to do so, he and Fust reached a new agreement, under which Gutenberg received another similar loan and the financier became a partner in the enterprise. At that time Gutenberg already printed with movable type, thus making the idea conceived in Strassburg a reality in Mainz. A valuable assistant to Gutenberg was his young employee and disciple Peter Schoeffer (c. 1425–1502), who joined the firm in 1452. In spite of their successes, the relationship between Gutenberg and Fust took a bad turn. Fust sued Gutenberg for two thousand guilders, and in 1455 the partnership was dissolved. Fust won the court action, thereby acquiring Gutenberg's materials and tools, and went into partnership with Schoeffer, who was his son-in-law.

Gutenberg's Mainz printshop may have contained as many as six printing presses. There is no way to know how many works Gutenberg produced, however, because tracing printed works of the fifteenth century is difficult. Also there are no surviving texts with Gutenberg's name on them. Nevertheless, historians believe that Gutenberg printed the Vulgate, the official Latin translation of the Bible. More than two hundred copies of the Vulgate were released during 1454 and 1455, some on calfskin, known as vellum, and the others on paper. Each page was composed of forty-two lines of print. For this reason, the Vulgate is known as the Forty-Two-Line Bible, but is also called the Gutenberg Bible or the Mazarin Bible. The work stands as the crowning achievement of many years of collaboration by the Gutenberg-Fust-Schoeffer team. One might expect that such an experimental "first book" would be crude and error filled. On the contrary, the forty-two-line Bible is a work of near perfection. The Gothic type is sharp and clear and the right hand margins are straight. Many of the copies were beautifully illuminated (illustrated with brightly colored paint) by hand in the spaces left by the printer for capital letters and headings. This process had been perfected during the Middle Ages (c. 400–1400) in the production of manuscripts.

As was true for much of Gutenberg's life, the inventor did not receive credit for his work. When the first finished copies of the Vulgate were published in early 1456, Guten-

## An important invention

Johannes Gutenberg perfected the method of manufacturing moveable lead-based type that met the precise and exacting the requirements for printed books. He apparently experimented with many materials in his attempt to make printing more efficient. He worked out a system of typecasting each letter of the alphabet individually with an engraved steel punch and matrix (mold) box. His formulas for both lead type and ink could still be used today. For the type he used an alloy (blend) of 80 percent lead, 5 percent tin, and 15 percent antimony. For the ink he used a mixture of linseed oil, varnish, and lampblack (carbon produced by burning oil in a lamp). Book pages were printed on either calfskin or on paper, which was cheaper. The printing press changed the course of Western civilization, and represented one of the most influential inventions in human history.

berg—undoubtedly the main creator of the work—no longer belonged to the partnership. The cost of production apparently exceeded the profits from sales, and Gutenberg was already being sued by Fust. Fust continued printing successfully with Gutenberg's equipment and also with machinery improved by Schoeffer. In the meantime Gutenberg had to start all over again. It is believed that the fruit of his work in these years is the Thirty-Six-Line Bible and the famous *Catholicon,* a kind of encyclopedia. Again, as Gutenberg never put his name on any of his works, assigning the printing to him is merely guesswork.

## Lives in poverty

In 1462 Fust's printing office was set on fire and Gutenberg and other craftsmen suffered losses as well. As a result of this disaster many typographers left Mainz and settled in other areas, where their carefully guarded secrets of printing began to spread. Gutenberg remained in Mainz, but he was again reduced to poverty. He requested the archiepiscopal (church district) court for a sinecure, an office given by the church that requires little or no work and provides a salary. Guttenberg's request was granted in 1465, and his post at the

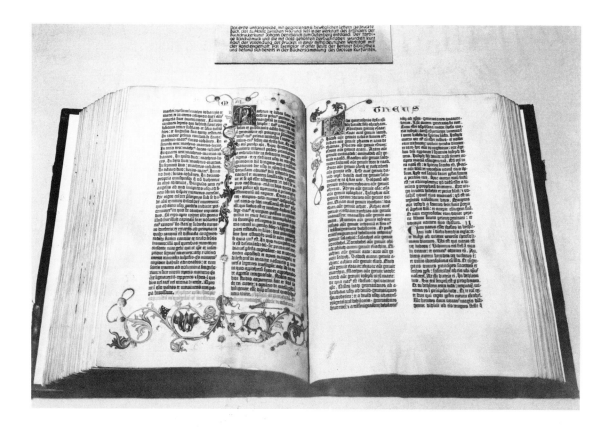

Johannes Gutenberg printed the Vulgate Bible, also known as the Gutenberg Bible, on his new invention called the printing press. ©*Bettmann/Corbis. Reproduced by permission of Corbis Corporation.*

court brought him some economic relief. Although Gutenberg continued his printing activities, works from this final period in his life are unknown because of lack of identification.

Reportedly, Gutenberg became blind in his last months, while he was living partly in Mainz and partly in the neighboring village of Eltville. He died in Saint Victor's parish in Mainz on February 3, 1468, and was buried in the church of the Franciscan convent in that town. His physical appearance is unknown, though there are many imaginary depictions of his face and figure, including statues erected in Mainz and Strassburg. In 1900 the Gutenberg Museum was founded in Mainz with an attached library that contains objects and documents related to the invention of typography.

## Gutenberg has great influence

Gutenberg's work in the development of the printing press was in many ways a turning point in the history of

Western civilization. The spread of printing had a limited effect on the Italian Renaissance of the fifteenth century, but it influenced cultural and commercial developments in northern and western Europe in the sixteenth century. During the last half of the fifteenth century, printshops, often staffed with master printers of German origin, appeared in many cities and towns in western Europe. The availability of printed books fundamentally changed the methods by which students, scholars, and other educated people stored, retrieved, and shared information. Gutenberg's invention guaranteed that information could be reproduced accurately, quickly, and cheaply. The manuscript and oral culture of medieval Europe shifted to the visual world of the printed page. Previously, handwritten or copied manuscripts had no punctuation or visual clues for paragraph structure, so they had to be read out loud or memorized. When the shift from hand-copied manuscript to the printed page occurred, there was less need to memorize texts or to read them aloud.

One result of the broad distribution of printed materials was the censorship of books. This practice was unnecessary in the limited world of the scribe (a person who copies texts), but it became common in the centuries following the development of printing. Although the printing press had little impact on the Italian Renaissance, many of the books produced in the first fifty years of printing were works of ancient Greeks and Romans that had been revived by fifteenth-century scholars. Also popular were late-medieval and early Renaissance writers such as the poets **Petrarch** (1304–1374; see entry) and Giovanni Boccaccio (1313–1375). Writing and composing new and original works for the printing press became common in the first several decades of the sixteenth century. Another new use of printing was the production of maps relating to the discoveries in the New World (the European term for the Americas). Accurate maps were essential to Europeans in understanding the new world.

Although information about Gutenberg's life is lacking, there is enough evidence to show that he deserves the acclaim he has received from the beginning of the age of print to the present. Gutenberg focused on and solved many complex problems of printing. His first major effort of book printing with moveable type, the forty-two line Bible, will remain a remarkable product of a revolutionary invention, the Gutenberg press.

# For More Information

## Books

Burch, Joann Johansen. *Fine Print: A Story about Johann Gutenberg.* Minneapolis: Carolrhoda Books, 1991.

Fisher, Leonard Everett. *Gutenberg.* New York: Macmillan, 1993.

Krensky, Stephen. *Breaking into Print: Before and After the Invention of the Printing Press.* Boston: Little, Brown, 1996.

## Web Sites

*The Gutenberg Bible.* [Online] Available http://prodigi.bl.uk/gutenbg/, January 3, 2002.

"Gutenberg, Johannes." *Famous People in Printing History.* [Online] Available http://www.ssc.cc.il.us/acad/career/depts/technology/ppt/whatsup/trivia/gutenbrg.htm, April 5, 2002.

*Gutenberg Museum.* [Online] Available http://www.gutenberg.de/, April 5, 2002.

# Henry VIII

**Born: June 28, 1491**
**Greenwich, England**
**Died: January 28, 1547**
**London, England**

**King**

Henry VIII is best known today as the king who discarded—or beheaded—his wives because they did not give him a male heir. He is also famous for defying the pope (the supreme head of the Roman Catholic Church). As a consequence of the pope's refusal to grant Henry a divorce from his first wife, Henry withdrew from the Roman Catholic Church and created the Church of England. Henry was also a great supporter of the English Renaissance. Although his daughter, **Elizabeth I** (1533–1603; see entry), is usually associated with the height of English culture, Henry set the stage by encouraging new humanist ideas that were being brought from Italy in the sixteenth century. (Humanism was a literary and scholarly movement based on the revival of ancient Greek and Roman culture that was the basis of the Renaissance.)

" ... if he were still free he would choose her in preference to all others."

*Henry VIII, upon marrying Catherine of Aragon.*

## Needs a male heir

Henry VIII was the second son of the first Tudor family ruler, King Henry VII (1457–1509; ruled 1485–1509), and his wife, Elizabeth of York. An excellent student as a child, he

**Henry VIII.**

learned Latin, Spanish, French, and Italian and studied mathematics, music, and theology. He became an accomplished musician and played several instruments. He composed hymns, ballads, and two masses (musical compositions used in Roman Catholic worship services). He also liked hunting, wrestling, and jousting. Henry VIII's older brother, Arthur (1486–1502), was originally the heir to the English throne. However, Arthur died in 1502, only a year after he married Catherine of Aragon (1485–1536), the daughter of the Spanish monarchs (kings and queen who has sole ruling power) Ferdinand II of Aragon (1452–1516; ruled 1479–1516) and Isabella I of Castile (1451–1504; ruled 1474–1504). The marriage was intended to forge an alliance between England and Spain, the most powerful kingdom in Europe at the time. Upon the death of Henry VII on April 21, 1509, Henry VIII took the throne of a peaceful kingdom. He married Catherine of Aragon on June 11, and thirteen days later they were crowned at Westminster Abbey. He enthusiastically remarked to his father-in-law that he loved Catherine so much that if he were single he would still choose her over other women.

Henry and Catherine remained happily married until 1527, but they had not had a male heir, despite the queen's numerous pregnancies. Only a daughter, Mary (1516–1568; ruled as Mary I, 1553–58), lived more than a few days. At that time the Salic Law prohibited a woman from serving as a monarch, so the king needed a son if he wanted to retain the Tudor family's hold on the throne. During this period Henry was devoted to the Roman Catholic Church (then the only Christian religion in Europe) and the pope. He joined the Holy League, an alliance headed by Pope Julius II (1443–1513; reigned 1503–13), which sought to prevent the French from acquiring territory in Italy. In 1513 Henry invaded northern France and personally commanded English troops at the famous Battle of the Spurs near the town of Thérouanne. The battle was given this name because of the speed with which the French drove their horses into retreat. England then acquired control of Thérouanne and another town, Tournai. Henry was not consulted when the treaty was signed, however, and he benefited less than he had expected. As a result he dismissed his chief ministers, who had been carried over from his father's reign. He gave control of the government to Thomas Wolsey (c. 1475–1530), a churchman who was also lord chancellor (head government official), archbishop (head of a church district) of York, and a cardinal (a church official ranking directly below the pope). Henry also supported the Catholic Church against the reform efforts of the German priest **Martin Luther** (1483–1546; see entry) who, in 1517, initiated the movement that became the Protestant Reformation. When Henry wrote *The Defense of the Seven Sacraments,* the pope expressed his appreciation by giving him the title "Defender of the Faith."

## Seeks divorce, brings Reformation

By 1527 it had become apparent that Catherine would bear no more children, and Henry became concerned about who would succeed him as king. Determined to continue the Tudor dynasty, he did not believe the English people would accept his daughter Mary, his only heir, as their monarch. Henry thus began to seek a divorce from Catherine so he could marry a younger woman who might give him a son. At about that time he fell in love with Anne Boleyn (c. 1507–1536), a lady-in-waiting (personal attendant) at Catherine's court, and he wanted to make her his wife. Henry mistakenly believed that it was a woman's fault if she did not bear a male child.

Henry and Wolsey appealed to Pope Clement VII (1478–1534; reigned 1523–34) for an annulment (declaration that a marriage is invalid) and permission for the king remarry. Under ordinary circumstances the pope would have granted such a request: Renaissance popes engaged extensively in politics, and Henry had gained the favor of the papacy (office of the pope). But Catherine opposed the divorce, as did her nephew, **Charles V** (1500–1558; see entry), king of Spain and Holy Roman Emperor. The pope did not feel that he could oppose Charles on the divorce since emperor's troops had sacked (robbed and burned) Rome, the seat of the Roman Catholic Church, in 1527, and Clement wanted Charles's support in other political matters. In mid-1529 the pope did arrange to have the divorce tried by Wolsey and Lorenzo Campeggio (1474–1539), an Italian cardinal, in London. In the end, the case was moved back to Rome and no verdict was reached. As a result, the irate king dismissed Wolsey and summoned what came to be known as the Reformation Parliament (ruling body of Great Britain). Wolsey was allowed to retain his position as archbishop of York, but he was forbidden to meddle in politics. When he was found to be corresponding with the French, he was summoned to London. Wolsey probably would have been executed had he not died a natural death in 1530.

For several years the king and Parliament were content with measures that destroyed the independence of the Catholic Church in England. For instance, the Conditional Restraint of Annates, which was enacted in 1532, put financial pressure on the papacy. By the beginning of 1533 Henry had a new chief minister, Thomas Cromwell (c. 1485–1540), and a new archbishop of Canterbury, Thomas Cranmer (1489–1556). Cromwell suggested that England should break ties with the Roman Catholic Church so that the archbishop rather than the pope could grant the divorce. Cranmer was eager to assist. So in January 1533 Henry married Anne Boleyn, even though he was still married to Catherine. By that time Anne was pregnant, and her pregnancy was causing considerable controversy at court. A few months later Parliament passed the famous Act in Restraint of Appeals, which said that no judicial decisions made in England could be appealed in Rome. In fact, the measure went even further by stating that the papacy had no jurisdiction in England. The following May, Cranmer granted Henry's divorce from Catherine and approved the marriage to Anne. In September, Anne bore Henry's second daughter, Elizabeth (1533–1603; ruled as Elizabeth I, 1558–1603).

The Protestant Reformation in England thus sprang from political manipulation and was imposed by the government. Elsewhere in Europe, reform was achieved through protest movements staged by the people, who demanded religious freedom through changes in their governments. The English Parliament continued to determine the course of religion, passing acts that named Henry VIII the Supreme Head of the Church, cut off payments to the papacy, regulated doctrine (church teachings), and ordered dismantling of monasteries (houses for male members of Catholic religious orders) and convents (houses for female members of Catholic religious orders) in the kingdom. Many people regretted these actions, some of which forbade the worship of popular saints and ordered the destruction of religious images. Reform was welcomed by others who believed the Catholic Church had become corrupt.

## Henry Closes Monasteries

One of the most important events of Henry VIII's reign was the closing of monasteries. At the beginning of the Tudor era the religious houses owned as much as one-fourth of all land in England. These estates had been given or bequeathed (granted in wills) to monks by religiously devout men and women in exchange for prayers for their souls after they died. Although the monasteries were reported to be corrupt, many historians believe Parliament used this as an excuse to order the smaller houses closed in 1536. Residents were allowed to transfer to larger houses that remained open or to renounce (refuse to obey) their vows. Most chose to renounce their vows. The great abbeys (churches connected with monasteries) were suppressed one by one in the next few years. A second statute, passed in 1540, legalized these closures and mandated the seizing of all remaining property. Former monastic possessions were managed by a new financial bureau, the Court of Augmentations. The court paid small pensions (financial allowances for retired people) to the former monks and nuns, and larger ones to the former abbots and priors (heads of monasteries) who had cooperated in the closing of their houses. By the time of Henry VIII's death in 1547, most of the monastic land had been sold to noblemen and members of the gentry. These people would thus profit from the continuation of the Reformation.

The loss of the monasteries was felt in various ways. Earlier they had been great centers of learning and the arts, but now the great monastic libraries were divided and sent to other locations. Some collections remained in cathedrals that had earlier been associated with monasteries, like Canterbury and Dudiam, and others were acquired by the universities of Oxford and Cambridge or by private collectors. Much of the wealth seized from the religious houses was spent on warfare.

## Beheads two wives

In 1536 Henry came to believe that Anne Boleyn had not been faithful to him. She was charged with adultery (having a sexual relationship outside of marriage) and beheaded at the Tower of London (a prison for royalty and the nobility). Henry then married his third wife, Jane Seymour (c. 1509–1537), who succeeded in giving him a male heir, Edward (1537–1553; ruled as Edward VI, 1547–53), in 1537. She died a few months later from complications of childbirth. The grief-stricken king remained single until 1540, when Cromwell persuaded him to marry Anne of Cleves

(1515–1557), the sister of a minor ruler of Germany. The goal was to forge a Protestant alliance that could be useful if the papacy and the Catholic states of Europe decided to make war on England. One sight of Anne, however, convinced Henry he had been deceived by reports about her attractive appearance and by a flattering portrait of her that he had commissioned. Shortly after Cranmer performed the marriage ceremony he began to arrange a divorce.

In 1540 Henry married his fifth wife, Catherine Howard (c. 1520–1542), who was Anne Boleyn's cousin and who shared Anne's fate. Catherine was charged with adultery and beheaded in 1542. Neither she nor the king's last wife, Catherine Parr (1512–1548), bore him children. At one time or another both of his daughters, Mary and Elizabeth, had been declared illegitimate (born out of wedlock). Shortly before his death, however, Henry drafted a will stating that the throne might pass in the normal order to all of his children, Edward, Mary, and Elizabeth. When Henry died in 1547 Edward was proclaimed King Edward VI, although he was only nine years old. Henry's wives Anne of Cleves and Catherine of Parr both outlived him.

Following the break with the Catholic Church, Henry and his advisers grew more and more concerned about the Catholic countries—primarily Spain and France—on the continent of Europe. They feared that Catholic nations would form an alliance and declare war on England in an effort to eliminate both the king and his Protestant church. Henry's government seized vast sums of money from the Catholic Church, especially the dissolved religious houses, but there were still not enough funds to meet military expenses. Taxation by the Parliament reached new heights in the 1540s, and expenditures on the navy and new fortifications were unprecedented. A second invasion of France in 1543, coupled with a campaign against Scotland, was costly but brought no real benefits.

## Supports Renaissance

The Italian Renaissance reached England during the early years of Henry's reign, and he became the true Renaissance prince. Handsome, dashing, well educated in classical

**Henry VIII surrounded by his six wives, clockwise from top, Anne of Cleves, Catherine Howard, Anne Boleyn, Catherine of Aragon, Catherine Parr, and Jane Seymour.** *Reproduced by permission of Hulton Archive.*

Latin and theology (religious philosophy), he was willing to spend money on learning and the arts. Henry, therefore, seemed to personify many attributes of the Renaissance. In 1520 great pageantry, which was characteristic of the most prominent Renaissance courts, adorned the meeting between Henry and **Francis I** (1494–1547; see entry), the Renaissance king of France, at the Field of the Cloth of Gold in France. The great humanist **Thomas More** (1478–1535; see entry)

## Hans Holbein, Court Painter

The German painter Hans Holbein the Younger (c. 1497–1543) was one of the best-known portraitists of the northern Renaissance. He still ranks among the great portrait painters in European art history. He is particularly famous as court painter for King Henry VIII. He painted portraits of Henry; two of the king's wives, Jane Seymour and Anne of Cleves; and Princess Christina of Denmark, to whom Henry unsuccessfully proposed. Holbein also did portrait paintings, drawings, and miniatures of various members of the court, including the French ambassador and his house guest, the Bishop of Lavour. Painted in 1533 and titled *The Ambassadors,* the double portrait includes the haunting image of a skull that serves as a contrast to youth, intellect, and good health. Other portrait subjects were the humanist Thomas More and young German merchants of the Hansa (trading organization) headquarters, or "Steelyard," in London.

Holbein's portraits were cherished by their owners. Yet before the advent of color photography in the twentieth century, when copies of his works were reproduced, he was relatively unknown. Holbein was not honored in Germany primarily because he moved first to Switzerland and later to England. Beginning in the twentieth century, however, exhibitions of the painter's works were held in Europe and the United States.

served as his lord chancellor (chief secretary) in the 1530s. (Henry had More beheaded when he would not acknowledge the king's supremacy over the pope.) The German artist Hans Holbein (c.1497–1543; see accompanying box) was Henry's court painter, and the English scholar Thomas Elyot (c. 1490–1546) was one of his secretaries. The Renaissance palace at Hampton Court, originally built by Thomas Wolsey, was taken over by Henry after Wolsey's fall and was the scene of many splendid entertainments. Saint Paul's School was founded early in Henry's reign by John Colet (c. 1466–1519), the learned dean (head) of Saint Paul's Cathedral. It was the first grammar school to provide rigorous instruction in the classical languages. The Latin grammar written for Saint Paul's by William Lily was the first text of classical Latin (the language used by ancient Romans). Elyot's dictionary (1538) was the first to provide English equivalents for all the words in the classical Latin vocabulary.

Less attractive features began to surface during the second half of Henry's reign. He proved to have limited intellectual abilities, and he was unwilling to give sufficient attention to the details of government. He was often unfaithful to his closest friends, even ordering the executions of two wives and two of his ministers. In his last years he did remain loyal to Catherine Parr and Thomas Cranmer, both of whom were accused of holding extreme religious views. In spite of his shortcomings, Henry was a popular king. Even at the end of his life, when he had become ill, obese, and tyrannical, he commanded the affection and respect of the English people.

## For More Information

### Books

MacDonald, Alan. *Henry VIII and His Chopping Block*. New York: Scholastic, 1999.

Weir, Allison. *Henry VIII: The King and His Court*. New York: Ballantine Books, 2001.

### Video Recordings

*The Private Life of Henry VIII*. Los Angeles: Embassy Home Entertainment, 1986.

*A Man for All Seasons*. Burbank, Calif.: RCA/Columbia Pictures Home Video, 1985.

### Web Sites

"Henry VIII." *Britannica.com*. [Online] Available http://www.britannica.com/eb/article?eu=40871&tocid=0&query=henry%20viii, April 5, 2002.

"Henry VIII." *History Channel*. [Online] Available http://www.thehistorychannel.co.uk/classroom/alevel/henry1.htm, April 5, 2002.

"Henry VIII." *Image Gallery*. [Online] Available http://www.tudorhistory.org/henry8/gallery.html, April 5, 2002.

*The Six Wives of Henry VIII*. [Online] Available http://www.larmouth.demon.co.uk/sarah-jayne/wives/wives.html, April 5, 2002.

# Ignatius of Loyola

**c. 1491**
**Guipuzcoa, Spain**
**July 31, 1556**
**Rome, Italy**

**Religious leader, founder of Jesuits**

"The safest and most suitable form of penance seems to be that which causes pain in the flesh but does not penetrate to the bones, that is, which causes suffering but not sickness."

*Ignatius of Loyola in* Spiritual Exercises, *quoted in* The Columbia World of Quotations. *[Online] Available http://www.bartleby.com/66/ 17/47917.html, April 5, 2002.*

**Ignatius of Loyola.**
*Painting by Peter Paul Rubens.*
*©Bettmann/Corbis.*
*Reproduced by permission of Corbis Corporation.*

Ignatius Loyola was the principal founder of the Society of Jesus (known as the Jesuits), a Roman Catholic order for men. Prior to having a spiritual awakening, Ignatius was a vain and worldly young soldier who loved a life of adventure. In 1521, at the Battle of Pamplona in Spain, he suffered serious injuries and, while recuperating, turned his mind to religion. During the next two decades he wandered penniless through Europe, made a pilgrimage (religious journey) to Jerusalem (site of the life and teachings of Jesus Christ, the founder of Christianity), and studied for the priesthood in Paris. During this time he gathered a growing number of followers and wrote *Spiritual Exercises*. An outline of methods of prayer and religious self-discipline, *Spiritual Exercises* became the handbook of the Jesuits. Ignatius's frequent visions of Jesus and Mary (Jesus's mother) also enhanced his reputation for saintliness. The Jesuits, which he founded in 1540, spread throughout Europe, gaining great political and religious influence. The order became a prominent force in the Catholic Reformation (also called the Counter Reformation) a reform movement within the Roman Catholic Church.

## Embarks on religious life

Ignatius was born into a noble family in Guipuzcoa, part of the Basque country on the Spanish side of the Pyrénées Mountains. Baptized Iñigo de Oñaz y Loyola, he adopted the name Ignatius in about 1537, in honor of Saint Ignatius (died c. A.D. 110) of Antioch, an early Christian martyr (one who sacrifices his or her life for a cause). After receiving a limited education, he became a soldier. His brief military career ended in 1521 when he was wounded in battle at Pamplona, Spain, during the Italian Wars (a conflict between France and Spain over control of Italy; 1494–1559). His fellow soldiers, recognizing their position as hopeless, had urged their commander to surrender. Ignatius's passionate appeals for a heroic defense changed the commander's mind. Ignatius then led the soldiers into battle until a cannonball hit him in the legs, smashing the right and gashing the left. When he fell, the Spanish surrendered. The French victors knew Ignatius by reputation, so they took good care of him. They did what they could to set his bones and bandage his wounds, then sent him to his family castle in Loyola to recover.

While recuperating, Ignatius had a series of religious experiences that changed the course of his life. He wanted to pass the time reading romances, but he found only books on the lives of the saints. He turned to them for lack of anything more exciting to read. Ignatius remembered later that his worldly daydreams had left a bitter aftertaste, whereas his religious reveries had filled him with joy. He concluded that the first pleasures came from the devil, the second from God. During this period of enforced meditation he made plans for a pilgrimage to Jerusalem. First, however, he learned that his bones were not setting properly. Rather than go through life disfigured and limping, he ordered that the bones be rebroken, a bone spur sawn off, and the bones reset, despite the incredible pain and the risk of infection.

During his recovery, Ignatius began a program of asceticism (strict self-denial) for which his Jesuit followers later honored him. He sometimes went days at a time without food and walked barefoot in winter. He deliberately neglected his long hair, which had once made him proud, until it was matted and filthy. He wore a hair shirt (garment made of rough animal hair worn next to the skin) and sometimes a nail-studded belt turned inward to his body. The effect of these torments was to weaken him and give him a pale and haggard appearance, which terrified both strangers and acquaintances. It also caused him lifelong stomach problems.

Ignatius lived for a time in Manresa, Spain, where he prayed six or more hours a day and spent a few hours a day begging for alms (money or food). He also worked in hospitals, caring for the poor. He had sold all his property and given away the proceeds to the poor. As a local nobleman, however, Ignatius was still well known in the community. His social status, along with his growing reputation for spirituality, led to frequent invitations to nobles' houses to dine and to give religious instruction. He refused to stay with the nobility, however, and retired to humble lodgings to sleep.

## Begins writing *Spiritual Exercises*

Ignatius tried to confess and do penance (an act to show sorrow or repentance) for all the sins of his earlier life. When he found he had committed so many sins that he could not count them all them, a priest suggested writing them out. Beginning in 1522 he spent a year in seclusion at the small town of Mansera outside Barcelona. During this time he put his ideas on paper, forming the background of *Spiritual Exercises,* which was published in 1548. This short but influential book outlines a thirty-day regimen (systematic plan) of prayer and self-abasement (acts of self-denial and punishment) that focuses on devotion to God.

In 1524 Ignatius set out to visit Jerusalem. At Barcelona, Spain, he persuaded the captain of a ship bound for Italy to take him on board, though he had no money for his passage. He took food only reluctantly, seeing starvation during the voyage as another opportunity for self-denial. After begging in Italy, he took a ship from Venice to Cyprus, then from Cyprus to Syria. From there he walked to Jerusalem to visit the Christian holy places, which were under the control of Muslim Turks (inhabitants of Turkey who followed the Islam religion). Ignatius asked the few Christian guardians of the holy places to permit him to remain near the sites of Jesus's life and death. Fearful that his militant Christian zeal would cause problems, they denied his request. After a farewell visit to the Mount of Olives to see what were alleged to be Jesus' footprints, Ignatius tried to find passage home "for the love of God" rather than for money. When the captains of both a large Venetian ship and a large Turkish ship would not accept him as a passenger, he boarded a smaller ship. The Venetian and Turkish ships sank a few days later in a Mediterranean storm, whereas the smaller ship carrying Ignatius weathered the storm and returned him safe to Venice. This good fortune on a hazardous voyage, as well as his experiencing several more visions of Jesus, became the basis of legends of his holiness. When Ignatius encountered hostility from soldiers and citizens in Italy, he went back to Spain.

## Imprisoned by Inquisition

Ignatius decided he needed a better education if he was to do his work effectively. He began to study Latin at Barcelona, then moved in 1526 to the recently founded university at Alcalá de Henares. Finally he spent a short time at the University of Salamanca. While Ignatius was at Alcalá de Henares and Salamanca, Catholic officials suspected him of being involved in the Protestant reform movement headed by the German priest **Martin Luther** (1483–1546; see entry). Holy Roman Emperor **Charles V** (1500–1558; see entry), who was also the king of Spain, was unable to stop the spread of Protestantism in Germany. He therefore used the Inquisition (church court established to find and punish heretics, or those who disobey church laws) to stamp it out in Spain. The Inquisition had been powerful and merciless in Spain since the late fifteenth century. Under its influence Muslim Spaniards (called Moriscos) were forced to convert to Christianity and Jews were expelled from the country in 1492. At autos da fé (pronounced awh-tohs deh FAY; acts of the faith), the Inquisition paraded sinners in public squares and burned condemned heretics at the stake.

Although Ignatius does not appear to have known about Luther, he was imprisoned without a trial or formal charges on several occasions. An usual prisoner, he made no effort to get a lawyer and refused to complain even when he was jailed on flimsy charges. On one occasion, the inmates of the prison broke out, and all but Ignatius and one of his followers escaped. The next day they were found in their cell with the door wide open. A growing number of townspeople in Alcalá, Barcelona, and Manresa, the towns he frequented, were learning of his spiritual gifts and his visions of Jesus and were becoming his followers. When several high-born women followed his example of turning to alms-begging, Ignatius had to endure allegations that he was a seducer (one who lures another person into sexual relations). Ignatius was usually found blameless despite his unconventional practices.

In 1528 Ignatius left Spain and went to the University of Paris, which was then the center of theological training in Europe. Again he lived on alms, begged in Flanders and England between academic sessions, and studied continuously. While in Paris, he met six of the men who were to form the nucleus of the Jesuits. At the same time, Ignatius had become seriously ill after fourteen years of fasting, flagellation (whipping oneself as a form of public penance), and other self-inflicted sufferings. Doctors told him that his only hope for recovery was to return home and rest. His followers in Paris bought him a donkey, and on it he undertook the 555-mile journey back to Spain. Arriving at Azpeitia without mishap in 1535, he rejected an invitation from his family to stay with them. Instead he went to the local poorhouse, where he again began to preach. By the middle of the year Ignatius was attracting huge crowds that listened to him preach each day. Several people later claimed he had performed miraculous cures, and many recalled that he had the gift of settling arguments between husbands and wives or fathers and sons. Ignatius left Spain shortly afterwards, never to return.

## Pope approves Society of Jesus

Ignatius was ordained a priest in 1537. He then requested that Pope Paul III (1468–1549) allow his group to make a pilgrimage to Jerusalem, where he hoped they might remain as hospital workers. The pope was delighted by the group's zeal and funded their journey. They planned to take a ship from the port of Venice to Syria, but Turkish pirates (ship robbers) in the Mediterranean prevented any pilgrim ships from setting sail that year. This was the only year in the past

half century that pilgrim ships did not leave Venice for Syria. The "Company of Jesus," as Ignatius and his followers now called themselves, took it as an omen (warning sign) that their future work did not lie in the Holy Land. Apart from taking short trips, Ignatius spent the rest of his life in Italy.

Rome, like much of Italy, was in need of both material and spiritual reform. The Protestant Reformation was a response to widespread and genuine abuses within the Catholic Church. Examples of such abuses are the buying and selling of Church offices, indulgences (the Roman Catholic Church practice of granting a partial pardon of sins in exchange for money), and relics, and the practicing of simony—the promotion of family members to high church positions by influential families. The popes were members of feuding families: the Sforzas, Borgias, Farneses, and others. Repeatedly since 1500, Italy had been swept by warring armies that brought famine and plague in their wake. In 1527, Rome itself had been sacked (robbed) and half burned down by a mutinous,

Ignatius of Loyola, founder of the Jesuits, surrounded by a few members of his order. *Reproduced by permission of Hulton Archive.*

or rebellious, army of the Holy Roman Emperor Charles V. As a result of Charles's attack on Rome, Pope Clement VII had to flee for his life.

Witnessing the disarray in Italy, Ignatius saw an opportunity to do his work closer to home. He invited his companions from around Italy to join him in Rome. The time had come, he told them, to establish a new Catholic order, the Society of Jesus, that differed from older orders, such as the Benedictines, Carthusians, Franciscans, and Dominicans. First, his group would be loyal to the pope. Second, they would not live a monastic life with regular hours of prayer and choral singing. Third, strict obedience to leaders of the order would be the foremost priority. (One of the oldest Jesuit tales is about a mortally ill novice on his deathbed, asking the novice-master for permission to die.) The organization's task was to act as "trumpeters of Christ." Members of the order were to be made strong and adaptable through prayer, self-surrender, and a very long training period. At first some influential Roman clergymen opposed Ignatius's plan, but the pope approved the establishment of the Society of Jesus as an order of the Catholic Church in 1540.

## Jesuits lead Catholic Reformation

In 1541 Ignatius was named the first superior general of the Jesuits. The order eventually grew from the original six followers to more than a thousand. One of the original members, Francis Xavier, became a missionary to India, Indonesia, and Japan (see accompanying box). Several Jesuits acted as experts at the Council of Trent (a series of meetings held to decide upon church reforms). Pierre Favre (Peter Faber; 1506–1546), another of Ignatius's earliest companions, was the first Jesuit to go to Germany. Rather than conflict, he advocated reconciliation with Protestants. Some Jesuits became missionaries in the New World (the European term for North and South America) and others went to Poland. The Jesuits also moved into the field of education, founding colleges in Italy, Portugal, the Netherlands, Spain, Germany, and India. These colleges became the basis of the Jesuit educational system that has continued to the present. By maintaining good relations with the popes, Ignatius was also able to improve

**Franicis Xavier**

Francis Xavier (1506–1552) was one of the six original followers of Ignatius of Loyola. He was born into a noble family at the castle of Xavier in the kingdom of Navarre (a region between France and Spain). Francis was a student at the University of Paris when he met Ignatius in the late 1520s. In 1534 Francis and the five other men took vows and formed the Society of Jesus under the leadership of Ignatius. The order was formally recognized by Pope Paul III in 1540.

When King João III of Portugal (1502–1557) issued a request for missionaries in Asia, Ignatius chose Francis to go to India. From 1542 until 1549 Francis ministered to Portuguese settlers and newly converted Indians in various parts of the country. He reportedly baptized more than ten thousand people in Travancore (a region in southwest India) alone. He also did mission work in Malaysia, Indonesia, and the Spice Islands. In 1549 he became the first Catholic missionary to Japan, where he stayed for two years. During that time he wrote a Japanese catechism (religious instruction in the form of questions and answers) in the Latin alphabet. In 1551 Francis became head of Jesuit missions in the region from the Cape of Good Hope (an extension of land at the tip of South Africa) to China and Japan. Hoping to bring Christianity to China, he set sail from Goa, India, in 1552. He accompanied the Portuguese ambassador's party. When they reached Malacca (Melaka) in Malaysia, however, the governor of that region would not let them continue on their journey. Francis then attempted to enter China secretly via the island of Chang-chuen (Saint John) near Macao (an island southeast of China). Arriving at Chang-chuen in late August, he became ill and died the following December.

During his work in Asia, Francis emphasized that it was essential for missionaries to learn the languages and customs of the people they hoped to convert. He also advocated training native people as clergymen. Francis was declared a saint in 1622, and in 1927 Pope Pius XI named him patron of all missions.

conditions in Rome. For instance, he set up Saint Martha's, a refuge (safe place) for reforming prostitutes (women who engage in sexual intercourse for money). For most of the last fifteen years of his life he worked a twenty-hour day, resting only to recover from increasingly severe illnesses. He finally died after a day of hard work in 1556. Ignatius was declared a saint in 1622. By that time the Jesuits had become the most powerful force of the Catholic Reformation.

# For More Information

## Books

*The Autobiography of St. Ignatius Loyola.* John C. Olin, editor, and Joseph F. O'Callaghan, translator. New York: Fordham University Press, 1993.

O'Malley, John W. *The First Jesuits.* Cambridge, Mass.: Harvard University Press, 1993.

Purcell, Mary. *The First Jesuit, St. Ignatius Loyola (1491–1556).* Chicago: Loyola University Press, 1981.

## Web Sites

"Loyola, Saint Ignatius of." *Britannica.com.* [Online] Available http://www.britannica.com/eb/article?eu=50361&tocid=0&query=ignatius%20loyola, April 5, 2002.

"St. Ignatius Loyola." *Catholic Encyclopedia.* [Online] Available http://www.newadvent.org/cathen/07639c.htm, April 5, 2002.

"Saint Ignatius of Loyola." *The Columbia World of Quotations.* [Online] Available http://www.bartleby.com/66/17/47917.html, April 5, 2002.

*The Spiritual Exercises of St. Ignatius of Loyola.* [Online] Available http://www.ccel.org/i/ignatius/exercises/exercises.html, April 5, 2002.

# James I
# (also James VI)

**June 19, 1566**
**Edinburgh, Scotland**
**March 27, 1625**
**Theobalds, England**

**King of Scotland and King of England**

King James I of England began his life as King James VI of Scotland, when he was merely an infant. As regents (interim rulers) ruled his kingdom, James was educated in the humanist tradition until he came of age. (Humanism was a movement to revive the culture of ancient Greece and Rome, which initiated the Renaissance.) His rather rough Scottish mannerisms and behavior were put to the test when he took over the throne of England after the death of **Elizabeth I** (1533–1603; see entry) in 1603. His political life was plagued by disagreements with his advisers and family, especially in regard to his relationship with Spain. James wrote a number of books, supported the arts, and patronized one of the best-known editions of the Bible (the Christian holy book), called the King James Version. Often manipulated by unqualified, inept advisers, James lived amidst court intrigue and power struggles. His inconsistent relationship with Parliament (main ruling body of Great Britain) prevented England from developing a stable form of government and a strong internal policy. Nevertheless, the actions of James I had a strong influence on subsequent leaders of England.

"A good king will not only delight to rule his subjects by the law, but even will conform himself in his own actions thereunto, always keeping that ground, that the health of the commonwealth be his chief law."

*James VI quoted in* King James VI and I, Political Writings, *edited by J. P. Somerville.*

James I.

173

Queen of Scots, was drawn into a plot against Elizabeth I, James did little to prevent Elizabeth from executing her in 1587. A year earlier, in 1586, James had married Anne of Denmark (1574–1619), a Protestant, to the immense joy of his subjects.

By 1592, however, feuds between the earl of Bothwell (James Hepburn, the man who helped James's mother murder his father) and other Catholic lords had reduced James to a virtual fugitive. In 1593 Bothwell took James captive, but was unable to keep him imprisoned. With the aid of the Scottish middle classes James took action against Bothwell, whom he accused of using witchcraft (use of spells to control supernatural forces) and the black arts (evil magic). The desperate Bothwell allied himself with other influential Catholic lords, but they had no real power against James. By the end of 1594 the position of the monarchy seemed secure.

James's sense of security was heightened by another event of 1594: the birth of a son and heir, Henry Frederick. During the next four years James continued to consolidate his position. In 1598 he published *The Trew Law of Free Monarchies,* which contained his ideas on church-state relations, the proper attitude of subjects toward their king, and the nature of divine right (the concept that a monarch is directly chosen by God). Within two years James had further refined his ideas in his most important work, *Basilikon Doron,* which he wrote as a book of advice for young Henry. For the rest of his life James was a prolific writer (see accompanying box).

## Sets stage for long reign

Elizabeth I died on March 24, 1603, and only eight hours after her death her nephew James was proclaimed king of England. While James succeeded Elizabeth peacefully, he inherited many of the problems that had been plaguing the nation for years: war with Spain, tensions within the church, a decline in patronage, domestic corruption, and the centuries-old bitterness between Scotland and England. James achieved success in several areas. In 1604 he signed a peace treaty with Spain, which soon created a boom in the British economy. That same year, at the Hampton Court Conference (a meeting called by James to discuss religious issues), James established the Church of England, or Anglicanism, as the

**Author and patron**

James was a prolific writer. As king of Scotland he wrote several works, including *The Trew Law of Free Monarchies* and *Basilikon Doron.* He continued writing after he took the English throne, producing political-theological texts, biblical interpretation, poetry, a discourse on the authority of judges, and parliamentary speeches and reflections. All of these works served James's sense of kingship.

He was also an active patron of the arts in England. Responding to his subjects' pent-up demands for patronage, he dispensed gifts, honors, titles, and positions within the church and state. The artistic efforts James supported were almost single-handedly responsible for the art collecting that came into vogue after 1604. Architecture, especially in the country, was widely supported and funded by James's court. The architect Inigo Jones (1573–1652) and the playwright Ben Jonson (1572–1637) were favorites of James and his followers. While patronage of the arts was not unusual for kings and queens, James's support of the arts, especially during times of financial troubles, was not always popular. His passion for tapestries, jewels, and luxurious dress drained the royal accounts and was often met with opposition, even in the court itself.

country's official religion. He also approved a new translation of the Bible, which first appeared in 1611.

In a sense, the events of the first two years of James's reign in England served to set the stage for the remainder of his twenty-two years on the throne. James had to make decisions on foreign policy, religion, finance, and governmental theory. He came into conflict with the English Parliament, especially with the House of Commons (lower branch of Parliament, which represents classes below the nobility), over England's relations with Scotland. In the first session of his first Parliament (1604) he gave speeches about his policies and about the privileges he had granted Parliament. This led Parliament to draft the "Apology of the Commons," in which the House of Commons equated their rights with those of all Englishmen. The Commons had suddenly assumed a new role. During this first Parliament, which lasted until 1610, opposition to the king focused mainly on his son, Henry, who was given his own household at the age of nine.

## Struggles with stubborn Parliament

As a youth James had been subjected to rather harsh treatment by ministers of the Presbyterian Church. Consequently, he wanted to keep control of the church in his own hands. He also preferred a highly ritualized form of worship, which seemed to indicate that he would have a somewhat lenient position regarding Roman Catholicism. The discovery of the Catholic conspiracy called the Gunpowder Plot to blow up the royal family and Parliament made James unwilling to deal with Catholics as a group. He was then forced to accept harsh measures against Catholics adopted by Parliament. James's subsequent efforts to relieve the limitations imposed on Catholics only made Parliament suspect his motives. Suspicion clouded James's relations with Parliament over several other issues as well. His attempts to unite England and Scotland as one kingdom were unsuccessful. His meddling in the dealings of the courts led him to quarrel with his own chief justice, Edward Coke (1552–1634), and to adopt a more extreme concept of his own rule. James's arbitrary raising of customs duties (taxes on goods) further outraged the Commons. Finally, his favoritism toward worthless courtiers, or members of his court, (Scottish and English alike) annoyed Parliament, angered Prince Henry, and irritated Queen Anne.

Always a lover of wealth and splendor, James had ongoing financial problems. By 1610 James's first Parliament came to an end amidst a severe financial crisis. With Parliament in retirement, government rested in the hands of James's favorite man of the moment, Robert Carr (1590–1645), earl of Somerset, and Carr's in-laws, the pro-Spanish Howard family. The pro-Spanish faction was briefly dealt a severe blow when Carr was named in a scandalous murder trial, that of Henry Howard, leader of the Spanish faction. Soon the king had a new favorite, George Villiers (1592–1628), who was not sympathetic to Spain. Yet James continued to seek relations with Spain, alienating Parliament. For two months neither the House of Commons nor the king would concede a point to the other. Finally, despite his growing need for money, James dissolved his unruly legislature.

In desperation, James turned to Don Diego Sarmiento (1567–1626), the Spanish ambassador (official representative in England) for financial assistance. The king's poverty gave him

An army camp during the Thirty Years' War. The conflict proved to be the greatest challenge of James's reign. *©Bettmann/ Corbis. Reproduced by permission of Corbis Corporation.*

no other choice, but his subjects saw this as further proof of his allegiance to Spain. James began to consider a Spanish bride for his son, Charles, Prince of Wales (1600–1649; later King Charles I, ruled 1625–49). James's first son, Henry, had died in 1612 and now Charles was in line for the throne. Although Sarmiento encouraged the king, they could not reach an agreement about a bride for Charles. Over the next decade James continued trying to arrange a Spanish marriage for Charles.

## Thirty Years' War brings challenge

In 1616 Villiers, now the duke of Buckingham, secured his position at court and became the focus of royal government. By 1618 he had destroyed the Howard family, and his power seemed to be complete. Buckingham's arrogance and rapid rise led to a quarrel with Prince Charles. James reconciled the two young men, and they soon became the best of friends. At the same time, James's health was now failing. He was badly crippled by gout (painful inflammation of the joints) and kidney stones (calcium deposits in the kidney), and he was not so alert mentally. At this unfortunate moment he was called upon to meet the greatest challenge of his reign: the outbreak of the Thirty Years' War (1618–48). The conflict started with a dispute over whether Bohemia (present-day Czechoslovakia) should be Protestant or Catholic. Bohemia was part of the vast Habsburg Empire, territory in central Europe controlled by the Habsburg family, who were Catholics and had branches in Austria and Spain. Bohemia was a Catholic country, but Protestants were demanding religious freedom.

James was still pursuing a pro-Spanish foreign policy in hopes of finding a wife, and a large dowry (property a woman brings to her marriage), for Charles. He also had visions of a union between Protestant and Catholic powers. In 1619 Austrian-Habsburg forces drove James's Protestant daughter, Elizabeth of Bohemia (1596–1662), and her husband, Frederick V (1596–1632), from their homeland in the Rhenish Palatinate (a region on the Rhine River in Germany). James believed that English support of intervention by the Spanish Habsburgs was the only way to settle the matter. Yet his subjects feared domination by Catholic Spain. They were also alarmed that James seemed to be deserting his own Protestant daughter and son-in-law by turning to Spain—their Catholic enemies. Reluctantly, and against the advice of Buckingham (who had now become pro-Spanish), James summoned Parliament in 1621. Since Parliament considered Spain the enemy, James and Buckingham knew they would face opposition because of their pro-Spanish policies. However, James realized he needed to seek additional funds from Parliament so he called it into session. Relations between the king and the lawmakers soon deteriorated. James denied virtually all of Parliament's privileges, and when the Commons protested, he dissolved Parliament altogether.

## Loses control in final years

The gulf between James and his subjects was now total. The king was bankrupt and dependent upon the goodwill of Spain, or so he thought. As he grew increasingly fee-ble, he lost control over Charles and Buckingham. The prince and the duke brought ridicule upon the king and the country by their hasty and unsuccessful attempt to arrange a marriage between Charles and the Spanish Infanta (daughter of the Spanish king). James's last Parliament was no more peaceful than his first had been. Again he and the House of Commons clashed over an alliance with Spain, but now the Commons was joined by the House of Lords (upper branch of Parlia-ment, which represents the nobility). In the end, the king gave in and support for Spain was withdrawn. James died soon thereafter, on March 27, 1625. He left behind an empty treasury, a discontented Parliament, and a son who would succeed him peaceably, though only for a little while.

## For More Information

### Books

Dwyer, Frank. *James I.* New York: Chelsea House, 1988.

Oliver, Isaac. *Art at the Courts of Elizabeth I and James I.* New York: Gar-land, 1981.

Sharpe, James. *The Bewitching of Anne Gunter: A Horrible and True Story of Deception, Witchcraft, Murder, and the King of England.* New York: Routledge, 2000.

### Web Sites

"James I." *Britannia.* [Online] Available http://www.britannia.com/history/monarchs/mon46.html, April 5, 2002.

"James I." *MSN Encarta.* [Online] Available http://encarta.msn.com/find/Concise.asp?ti=05A7D000, April 5, 2002.

# Ben Jonson

**June 11, 1572
in or near London, England
August 6, 1637
London, England**

**English playwright**

"For a good poet's made
as well as born."

*Ben Jonson,* To the Memory of
Shakespeare *quoted in*
Bartlet's Familiar Quotations,
*[Online] Available
http://www.bartleby.
com/100/, April 3, 2002.*

**Ben Jonson.**
*Photograph courtesy of
The Library of Congress.*

The English playwright and poet Ben Jonson is best known for his satiric comedies (plays based on criticism through the use of humor). An immensely learned man with an irritable and domineering personality, he was, next to **William Shakespeare** (1564–1616; see entry), the greatest dramatic genius of the English Renaissance. The Renaissance was a cultural revolution that began in Italy in the mid-1300s. It was initiated by scholars called humanists who promoted the human-centered values of ancient Greece and Rome. Humanist ideals were soon influencing the arts, literature, philosophy, science, religion, and politics in Italy. During the early fifteenth century, innovations of the Italian Renaissance began spreading into the rest of Europe and reached a peak in the sixteenth century.

## Becomes successful playwright

Ben Jonson was born on June 11, 1572, in or near London, England, and received his formal education at Westminster School. He did not continue his schooling, probably

A page of manuscript from the opening verse of Ben Jonson's *Ode to Himself*.

because his stepfather forced him to engage in the more practical business of bricklaying. Nevertheless, Jonson studied the classics (literary works by ancient Greek and Roman writers) throughout his active life. He began his theatrical career as a strolling player in towns throughout the country. By 1597 he had returned to London and had begun writing plays. Jonson's first piece of dramatic writing, *The Isle of Dogs,* was judged to be a "lewd" (indecent) work containing material

**Christopher Marlowe**

The English dramatist and poet Christopher Marlowe (1564–1593) was another important figure in the English Renaissance. He was the first English playwright to make significant advances in tragic drama. He was killed at age twenty-seven, and scholars speculate that if he had lived longer he would certainly have rivaled the dramatic genius of William Shakespeare and Ben Jonson.

Marlowe was born in Canterbury, England, in February 1564, about two months before Shakespeare. He received his early education at King's School in Canterbury and at age seventeen enrolled at Cambridge University, where he held a scholarship requiring him to study for the ministry. He received a bachelor of arts degree in 1584 and a master of arts degree in 1587. Toward the end of his stay at Cambridge he evidently aroused the suspicions of university authorities, who threatened to withhold his degree. The Queen's Privy Council (chief advisers of Queen Elizabeth I) intervened, however, and assured the authorities that Marlowe "had done Her Majesty good service." The nature of this service is still a mystery, but it is likely that Marlowe was involved in a secret espionage (spying) mission abroad.

Shortly after receiving his master's degree, Marlowe went to London. He soon became known for his wild behavior and unconventional ideas. In 1589 he was imprisoned for a time in connection with the death of a certain William Bradley, who had been killed in a violent quarrel in which Marlowe played an important part. Several times Marlowe was accused of being an "atheist" (one who does not believe in God) that was "seditious" (treasonous) and "slanderous" (damaging to a person' reputation). Jonson was imprisoned for this offense. In 1598 he was in more serious trouble. Having killed a fellow actor in a duel, he escaped hanging only by claiming right of clergy—that is, by reciting a few words of a religious nature in Latin, which was commonly known as "neck-verse."

In the same year Jonson's first major work, *Every Man in His Humour,* was performed by the Lord Chamberlain's Men, with Shakespeare taking the lead role. Called a "comedy of humors," the play features characters whose behavior is dictated by a dominating whim or affectation (pretense). It was followed by *Every Man out of His Humour* (c. 1599), *Cynthia's Revels* (1601), and *Poetaster* (1601). These three "comical

and a "blasphemer" (one who makes insulting statements about God or the church). One of his main accusers was fellow playwright Thomas Kyd (1558–1594). These charges led to Marlowe's arrest in 1593, but he died before his case was decided.

Marlowe was killed in a tavern fight on May 30, 1593. He was dining in the town of Deptford with a man named Ingram Frizer and two other men. In the course of an argument over the tavern bill, Marlowe wounded Frizer with a dagger. Frizer then seized the same dagger and stabbed Marlowe over the right eye. According to the coroner's inquest, Marlowe died instantly. Despite the unusual wealth of detail surrounding this fatal episode, there has been much speculation about the affair. It has been suggested, for example, that the deed was politically motivated and that Frizer (who was subsequently judged to have acted in self-defense) was simply acting as an agent for a more prominent person.

Marlowe's career as a poet and dramatist spanned a mere six years. Between his graduation from Cambridge in 1587 and his death in 1593 he wrote only one major poem (*Hero and Leander,* unfinished at his death) and six or seven plays. One play, *Dido Queen of Carthage,* may have been written while he was still a student. Marlowe's best-known tragedies are *Tamburlaine the Great* (1590), *Doctor Faustus* (1604), and *The Jew of Malta* (1633). In each of these plays he focused on a single character who dominates the action with his extraordinary strength of will. Shakespeare later perfected this form in his famous tragedies.

satires" represent Jonson's contribution to the so-called war of the theaters—a short-lived feud between rival theatrical companies. Jonson then wrote one of his most important works, the tragedy *Sejanus His Fall* (1603), which was admired by intellectuals but considered boring by average playgoers.

By 1604, before he had written his most famous works, Jonson had become known as the foremost writer of masques in England. A masque is a type of theater that dates back to antiquity, in which actors wear masks over their faces, which both disguises their true appearance and helps amplify their voices in large theaters. He continued writing masques throughout his career, frequently in cooperation with the famous architect Inigo Jones (1573–1652), who designed the stage sets and machinery (devices used to produce effects and move scenery). Jonson's dramatic genius was fully revealed for the first time in *Volpone* (1606), a satiric comedy that contains the playwright's harshest and most unrelenting criticism of human vice (wrongdoing). All the principal figures are named (in Italian) after animals suggestive of their characters. For example, Volpone is the cunning fox and Voltore is the ravenous vulture (bird of prey that feeds on dead animals). The main action turns on Volpone's clever scheme to cheat those who are as greedy as he but not nearly so clever. With the help of his servant Mosca, he pretends to be deathly ill. Each of the dupes (those who are tricked) is encouraged to believe that he may be designated heir to Volpone's fortune. They try to win his favor by presenting him gifts. Volpone is too clever for his own good, however, and is finally, betrayed by Mosca and exposed to the magistrates, or judges, of Venice. The punishment imposed on him, and on the self-seeking dupes as well, is unusually severe for a comedy. In fact, there is almost nothing in *Volpone* which provokes laughter.

## Career declines

The satire of Jonson's next three comedies is less harsh. *Epicoene, or the Silent Woman* (1609) features an elaborate plot built around a ridiculous character with an insane hatred of noise. In *The Alchemist* (1610) the characters are motivated more by vice than folly—particularly the vices of hypocrisy, or false virtue, and greed. Their punishment consists largely in their humiliating self-exposure. *Bartholomew Fair* (1614) has a relatively thin plot featuring a rich and varied collection of unusual characters. After *Bartholomew Fair*, Jonson's dramatic powers suffered a decline. Nonetheless, he remained an impressive and respected figure, especially in literary and intellectual circles. He was also idolized by a group of younger poets and playwrights who styled themselves as the "tribe of Ben."

Jonson's nondramatic writings included a grammar (rules for using language) of the English language (1640), a collection of notes and reflections titled *Timber, or Discoveries* (1640), and a large number of poems. After the death of King **James I** (1566–1625; see entry) in 1625, Jonson suffered a number of setbacks. His talents as a masque writer were not fully appreciated by the new king, so he was in less in demand and frequently short of money. After becoming paralyzed in 1628, Jonson was confined to his home in Westminster. He died nine years later and was buried with great ceremony in Westminster Abbey.

## For More Information

### Books

Harp, Richard, and Stanley Stewart, eds. *The Cambridge Companion to Ben Jonson*. New York: Cambridge University Press, 2000.

### Web Sites

*Bartlett's Familiar Quotations*. [Online] Available http://www.bartleby.com/100/, April 3, 2002.

"Ben Jonson." *TheatreHistory.com*. [Online] Available http://www.theatrehistory.com/british/jonson001.html, April 5, 2002.

Jokinen, Anniina. "Jonson, Ben." *Luminarium Profile*. [Online] Available http://www.luminarium.org/sevenlit/jonson/, April 5, 2002.

Jokinen, Anniina. "Marlowe, Christopher." *Luminarium*. [Online] Available http://www.luminarium.org/renlit/marlowe.htm, April 5, 2002.

"Jonson, Ben." *Encyclopedia.com*. [Online] Available http://www.encyclopedia.com/searchpool.asp?target=@DOCTITLE%20Jonson%20%20Ben, April 5, 2002.

# Johannes Kepler

**December 27, 1571**
**Weil, Swabia, Germany**
**November 15, 1630**
**Regensburg, Bavaria, Germany**

**Astronomer**

"For just as the eye is fitted for the perception of colors, the ear for sounds, so is man's mind created not for anything but for the grasping of quantities."

*Johannes Kepler.*

**Johannes Kepler.**
©*Bettmann/Corbis.*
*Reproduced by permission of*
*Corbis Corporation.*

The German astronomer Johannes Kepler was one of the chief founders of modern astronomy (study of celestial bodies, such as planets, stars, the Sun, and the Moon). A pivotal figure in seventeenth-century science, he made discoveries in astronomy and mathematics that spurred further developments. Many of his findings are still valid today. He is best known for his discovery of three basic laws underlying the motion of planets.

Johannes Kepler was born to a Lutheran family in the Catholic city of Weil in Swabia, Germany. In 1576 his family moved to Leonberg in the Protestant duchy (province) of Würtemberg. Kepler's grandmother raised him, and for many years he was a sickly child. At age thirteen he was accepted into a Lutheran theological seminary at Adelberg. Kepler wanted to become a theologian (a scholar who studies and teaches religion), and in 1589 he enrolled at the University of Tübingen to prepare for the ministry. There he was introduced to the theories of the Polish astronomer **Nicolaus Copernicus** (1473–1543; see entry), who proposed that the Sun, not the Earth, is the center of the universe.

## Writes important book

In 1594 Kepler interrupted his theological studies to accept a post as a mathematics teacher in the Protestant seminary at Graz (a city in present-day Austria). He also worked as the district mathematician. One of his duties was using astrology (a method of predicting future events according to the positions of planets and stars) to write an almanac, in which the main events of the coming year were predicted. His first almanac, published in 1596, was a great success. Two of his predictions—an invasion by the Ottoman Turks (inhabitants of the Ottoman Empire, a Muslim kingdom in Asia and North Africa) and a severe winter—came true and established his reputation as an astrologer. Kepler also spent his time studying problems in astronomy, working out theories of the circular orbits of planets. In 1596 he published *Mysterium cosmographicum* (Secret of the universe). His main thesis was that the distances between the planets in Copernicus's system were proportional to the five solids described by the ancient Greek philosopher Plato (c. 428–348 B.C.). Kepler saw this as proof of Copernicus's theory of a Sun-centered universe. In addition, he reflected on what made the planets move in their orbits. Although Kepler's thesis was incorrect, his book was important. It set forth many of the themes in astronomy that occupied him, including the belief that the universe could be described by simple mathematics. With *Mysterium cosmographicum* Kepler gained fame as an astronomer.

In 1597 Kepler married Barbara Muehleck, who had already been twice widowed. Of their five children, only one boy and one girl reached adulthood. Now that Kepler was a famous astronomer he came to the attention of Tycho Brahe (see accompanying box), the famous Danish astronomer who was the imperial mathematician at the court of the Holy Roman Emperor Rudolf II (1552–1612; ruled 1576–1612) in Prague (a city in present-day Czechoslovakia). Brahe invited Kepler to become his assistant, and in 1600 Kepler joined Brahe in Prague. Kepler returned to Graz the following June, but he found that Archduke Ferdinand of Styria (1578–1637), the future Holy Roman Emperor Ferdinand II (ruled 1619–37), was enforcing measures against Protestants. Kepler therefore had to leave Graz in spite of his social position. He rejoined Brahe in Prague, where he was one of many intellectuals gathered around Rudolf's court. When Brahe died the following year, Kepler was appointed his successor as imperial mathematician.

## Formulates laws

Kepler's first task was to prepare Brahe's collection of astronomical studies for publication. The goal was to establish definitive planetary tables in Rudolf's honor. The outstanding feature of Brahe's work was that he surpassed all other astronomers before him in making precise observations of the positions of stars and planets. Kepler tried to utilize Brahe's data in support of the circular orbits of planets. He was therefore forced to make one of the most revolutionary assumptions in the history of astronomy. He found that there was a difference of eight minutes of arc between his own calculations and Brahe's data. (An arc is the path of a celestial body above and below the horizon of the Earth. Minutes of arc is the length of time required for the body to move along its path.) This difference could be explained only if the orbit of Mars was not circular but elliptical (oval-shaped). This meant that the orbits of all planets were elliptical, a theory that became known as Kepler's first law. Kepler then developed his second law, which states that the line joining Mars to the Sun sweeps over equal areas in equal times in an elliptical orbit. He published these two laws in his lengthy discussion of the orbit of the planet Mars, *Astronomia nova* (New astronomy; 1609).

During his years in Prague, Kepler became interested in optics (scientific study of light). His *Ad Vitellionem paralipomena* (Supplement to Witelo), published in 1604, describes the process of vision, including the function of the retina (membrane that lines the eye), and discloses his inverse law of refraction (changes in density of light). In 1610 Kepler received news that the Italian astronomer **Galileo** (1564–1642; see entry) had perfected a telescope (an instrument used for viewing distant objects). He responded to Galileo's *Sidereus nuncius* (Starry messenger; 1610) with *Dissertatio cum nuncio sidereo* (Conversation with the starry messenger) in 1610 and *Dioptrice* (Dioptrics) in 1611. These two books discussed the optics of lenses, including the double convex (curving outward) lenses of the telescope.

In 1611 Rudolf stepped down from the throne. Kepler immediately looked for a new job because Protestants were being persecuted in Prague. He took the post of provincial mathematician in Linz the following year. By this time his

## Tycho Brahe

The Danish astronomer Tycho Brahe (1546–1601) made his first contribution to astronomy in 1572, when a supernova (explosion of a very large star) burst into view in the constellation (assemblage of stars) of Cassiopeia. Brahe was enthralled. The new star became brighter than the planet Venus and was visible for eighteen months. He described it with such detail in a book that the new star became known as "Tycho's star." The title of the book, *De Nova Stella* (Concerning the New Star), linked the term "nova" to all exploding stars. In this work Brahe revealed that he could not make a parallax measurement (angular distance in direction of a celestial body as measured from two points on Earth's orbit) for the nova, revealing that it was much more distant than the Moon. This was a crushing blow to the ancient Greek scholar Aristotle's teachings that the heavens were perfect and unchanging.

In 1577 a bright comet (a celestial body consisting of a fuzzy head surrounding a bright nucleus) was visible in the skies, and Brahe observed it with great care. Measurements showed that it, too, was farther away from the Earth than the Moon. Brahe came to the conclusion that the path of the comet was not circular but elongated, or stretched out. This meant it would have to pass through the "spheres" that carried the planets around the sky, which would be impossible unless the spheres did not exist. This concept was personally troubling to Brahe, who rejected Copernicus's Sun-centered theory because it violated Scripture (text of the Bible, the Christian holy book).

In 1576 Frederick II, king of Denmark, provided Brahe with an annual income and gave him a small island called Hveen (now Ven) off the southwest coast of Sweden. The king funded the building of the first real astronomical observatory in history. Brahe spent twenty years at Hveen, recording exceptionally accurate observations. His measurements were the most precise that could be made without the aid of a telescope. Brahe was relieved of his duties when Frederick II died in 1588. The astronomer moved to Prague, where he resumed his observations as the mathematician-astronomer to Holy Roman Emperor Rudolf II. Brahe employed Johannes Kepler, to whom he gave all his observations on the planet Mars. He assigned Kepler the task of preparing tables of planetary motion. This would turn out to be the most significant decision of Brahe's life. Kepler used the data to discover the three laws of the motions of planets.

wife and his favorite son, Friedrich, had died and only two of his children were still living. In 1613 Kepler married Suzanna Reuttinger, with whom he lived happily. His life in Linz was disrupted, however, when his aged mother was accused of being a witch. As a result of his contacts with theologians at Tübingen, Kepler was at least able to prevent her from being tortured during the investigation. She was later freed. In spite of these events, Kepler continued to do important work. His musings on the quantity of wine held in his barrels resulted in *Nova stereometria dolorium vinariorium* (New stereometrics of wine casks). It was published in 1615 and became an important development of calculus (method of mathematical calculation using special notation).

The work that Kepler considered the culmination of his studies was *Harmonice mundi* (Harmony of the world; 1618), in which he stated his third law. According to this law, the square of the period in which a planet orbits the Sun is proportional to the cube of its mean (average) distance from the Sun. (Square is a mathematical value obtained by multiplying a number by itself; also called raising to the second power. Proportional means having the same ratio, or relationship in size. Cube is a mathematical value obtained by taking a number three times as a factor.) Kepler based this theory on his conviction that God had created a perfectly balanced universe and had given humans a mind so that they could understand it.

## Identifies physical force

While in Linz, Kepler also wrote *Epitome astronomiae Copernicanae* (Epitome of Copernican astronomy), which was published in parts between 1618 and 1621. It was the first astronomical study that abandoned the idea of circles carrying the various planets in their orbits. Kepler thus raised the question of what kind of force was holding the planets in their paths. He concluded that it was a physical force consisting of "magnetic arms" that stretched out from the Sun. By identifying a physical force in the universe, Kepler laid the foundation for a relationship between physics and astronomy. In 1627, he published *Tabulae Rudolphinae* (Rudolfine Tables), a catalog of stars. This work added 223 stars to the 777 stars observed by Brahe. The tables were used by astronomers for the next century.

The last years of Kepler's life were unsettled. In 1626 the press where *Tabulae Rudolphinae* was being printed was

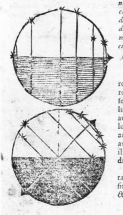

destroyed during a siege in the Thirty Years' War (1618–48; a political and religious conflict involving major European powers). He joined the court of Count Albrecht von Wallenstein (1583–1634) in the duchy of Sagan, Prussia, in 1628. Kepler had done a horoscope for Wallenstein in 1608, and in 1624 he did a more detailed chart in which he supposedly predicted Wallenstein's assassination in 1634. (Wallenstein was the commander of imperial forces in the Thirty Years' War. After trying to lead a revolt with trusted generals, he was dismissed by Emperor Frederick. Wallenstein was then assassinated by Irish and Scotch officers.) Although the count wanted Kepler's expertise in astrology, Kepler was unhappy in Sagan. He left for Prague in 1530 to collect the salary Emperor Frederick owed him for the *Tabulae Rudolphinae*. During the journey to Prague, Kepler died in Regensburg, Germany.

Before his death Kepler had written a work titled *Somnium* (Dream). He began to print it in Sagan, but it was not published until 1634. In the book he described how the solar system would appear to a person who took a trip to the Moon. *Somnium* is considered a forerunner of modern science fiction.

## For More Information

### Books

Banville, John. *Kepler, a Novel.* New York: Vintage, 1993.

Christianson, John Robert. *On Tycho's Island: Tycho Brahe and His Assistants, 1570–1601.* Cambridge University Press, 1999.

Kepler, Johannes. *The Harmony of the World,* translators E .J. Aiton, A. M. Duncan, J.V. Field. Philadelphia, Pa.: American Philosophical Society, 1997.

Voelkel, James R. *Johannes Kepler: And the New Astronomy.* New York: Oxford University Press Children's Books, 2001.

### Web Sites

*Kepler, Johannes—Kepler's Laws of Planetary Motion.* [Online] Available http://zebu.uoregon.edu/textbook/planets.html, April 5, 2002.

"Kepler, Johannes." *MSN Encarta.* [Online] Available http://encarta.msn.com/find/Concise.asp?ti=02F84000, April 5, 2002.

"Kepler, Johannes." *NASA Kepler Museum.* [Online] Available http://www.kepler.arc.nasa.gov/johannes.html, April 5, 2002.

Plant, David. *Kepler, Johannes—Kepler and the Music of the Spheres.* [Online] Available http://www.astrology-world.com/kepler.html, April 5, 2002.

# Index

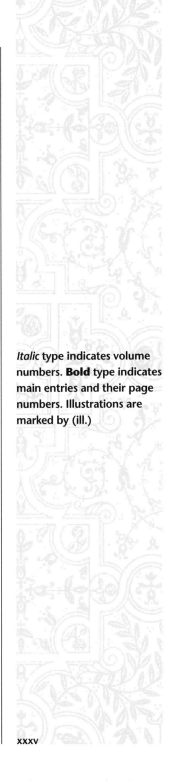